Building Games with Ethereum Smart Contracts

Intermediate Projects for Solidity Developers

Kedar Iyer

Chris Dannen

Apress®

Building Games with Ethereum Smart Contracts

Kedar Iyer
Brooklyn, New York, USA

Chris Dannen
Brooklyn, New York, USA

ISBN-13 (pbk): 978-1-4842-3491-4
https://doi.org/10.1007/978-1-4842-3492-1

ISBN-13 (electronic): 978-1-4842-3492-1

Library of Congress Control Number: 2018943122

Managing Director, Apress LLC: Welmoed Spahr
Acquisitions Editor: Louise Corrigan
Development Editor: James Markham
Coordinating Editor: Nancy Chen

Cover designed by eStudioCalamar

Cover image designed by Freepik (www.freepik.com)

Distributed to the book trade worldwide by Springer Science+Business Media New York, 233 Spring Street, 6th Floor, New York, NY 10013. Phone 1-800-SPRINGER, fax (201) 348-4505, e-mail orders-ny@springer-sbm.com, or visit www.springeronline.com. Apress Media, LLC is a California LLC, and the sole member (owner) is Springer Science + Business Media Finance Inc (SSBM Finance Inc). SSBM Finance Inc is a **Delaware** corporation.

For information on translations, please e-mail rights@apress.com, or visit www.apress.com/rights-permissions.

Apress titles may be purchased in bulk for academic, corporate, or promotional use. eBook versions and licenses are also available for most titles. For more information, reference our Print and eBook Bulk Sales web page at www.apress.com/bulk-sales.

Any source code or other supplementary material referenced by the author in this book is available to readers on GitHub via the book's product page, located at www.apress.com/9781484234914. For more detailed information, please visit www.apress.com/source-code.

Printed on acid-free paper

Table of Contents

About the Authors

Kedar Iyer is a software engineer who runs Emergent Phenomena, a blockchain consultancy. He is currently writing blockchain software as a member of the Everipedia team. He has a bachelor's degree in mechanical engineering from UCLA and has worked in the past with microsatellites, robotics, and multiple startups.

Chris Dannen is a cofounder and partner at Itcrative Capital, a large-scale cryptocurrency miner, investment manager, and private digital asset exchange. A self-taught programmer, he has written three technical books and holds one computer hardware patent. He was formerly the technical editor at *Fast Company*. He graduated from the University of Virginia and lives in New York.

About the Technical Reviewer

 **Massimo Nardone** has more than 23 years of experience in security, web/mobile development, and cloud and IT architecture. His true IT passions are security and Android.

He holds a master of science degree in computing science from the University of Salerno, Italy.

He currently works as chief information security officer (CISO) for Cargotec Oyj and is a member of ISACA Finland Chapter Board.

Massimo has reviewed more than 40 IT books for various publishing companies and is the coauthor of *Pro Android Games* (Apress, 2015).

Acknowledgments

Thank you to Chris Dannen and Solomon Lederer for getting me into blockchain and introducing me to the NYC blockchain community. To Nancy Chen and James Markham at Apress for putting together this book, and Chris for offering me the opportunity to write it. And to my parents and sister for being supportive of my odd career choices.

—Kedar

Thank you to my team at Iterative Capital for their hard work and support, and to Kedar for traversing the smoky parlors of Las Vegas to make the games in this book especially authentic.

—Chris

What Is Ethereum?

Ethereum is a trusted compute platform with a native currency built on top of a decentralized network. A global network of nodes works together to form a consensus on the state of a shared database.

If Bitcoin offers us a glimpse into the future of money, Ethereum offers the equivalent for private property, financial assets, legal contracts, supply chains, and personal data. Any digital unit that can be owned by someone can be stored in an Ethereum smart contract and transferred between owners without the need for a third party or middleman such as a bank, exchange, or central government.

Ethereum works by successively executing a series of transactions, each of which is a block of code. That code is written in a special language named Solidity. This is the language we will be exploring in this book.

We will start by getting set up (Chapter 2), deploying simple contracts (Chapter 3), and going over the basics of the Solidity language (Chapter 4). Then we will take a brief detour into the theory behind contract security (Chapter 5) and crypto-economics (Chapter 6) before spending the last half of the book walking through a series of sample projects (Chapters 7–11). By the end of this book, you will be comfortable reading and interpreting existing Solidity contracts and ready to write your own original Solidity code.

Prerequisites

Working with Ethereum and Solidity requires some knowledge of computer science concepts and prior experience with another programming language. You don't need to be an expert, though; just the basics will do.

Computing Concepts

The best resource for learning the basics of computer science is the Harvard CS50 lecture series on YouTube (www.youtube.com/user/cs50tv). It's a fast-paced, detailed course. If you can make it through all 10 weeks, by all means do, but the first five lectures will teach you enough to tackle Solidity.

For learning about networking, Linux, or security and hacking, check out the popular uploads for Eli the Computer Guy on YouTube (www.youtube.com/user/elithecomputerguy/videos?shelf_id=26&view= 0&sort=p). His videos are much more beginner-friendly than the CS50 lectures, so if you're looking for a soft intro to ease you in, this the place to start.

We will be using UNIX (Linux or Mac) command lines throughout the book. Instructions are given for how to make your Windows system compatible with our commands, but we recommend learning Linux if you can.

Networking and security are less important concepts to know, and you can make it through the book and become a Solidity developer without any prior knowledge of either. Networking is important in the Ethereum protocol under the hood, but is abstracted away at the application level, where we will be writing our code. Security is important because the amount of money passing through our contracts will make them lucrative targets. We spend an entire chapter discussing contact security (Chapter 5), but any additional knowledge you can obtain on the topic will serve you well.

Programming

Before diving into Solidity, you should have previous programming experience with another language. The closest language to Solidity is C, but it is neither beginner-friendly nor easy to set up. Your best bet for a simple programming introduction is Codecademy. The simplest language to learn is Python, and the simplest Codecademy course is <u>Learn Python</u> (`www.codecademy.com/learn/learn-python`).

JavaScript, while slightly more confusing with syntax, is still easy to learn and more relevant to Ethereum programming because it is used by most client software for interacting with the blockchain. We will be writing and issuing simple JavaScript scripts and commands in this book. The best resource for JavaScript is the Codecademy <u>Introduction to JavaScript</u> course (`www.codecademy.com/learn/introduction-to-javascript`).

Suggested Reading

This book is an intermediate-level programming book. Before starting with this book, consider that maybe you should be reading a different one.

Introducing Ethereum and Solidity by Chris Dannen (Apress, 2017) is a great book for getting you up to speed with all things Ethereum. If you just want to understand how Ethereum works without getting deep into the nuances of writing smart contracts, that's the book you should be reading.

In the Beginning...was the Command Line by Neal Stephenson (William Morrow, 1999) is the best book I've come across on the history and metaphysics of software. It reads like a novel, is far better written than this book, and if you're here for anything except learning Solidity, you should probably be there instead.

Protocols, Platforms, and Frameworks

Ethereum is both a protocol and a platform, but not a framework.

A *protocol* is a series of rules used to standardize communication over a network. Basic protocols such as IP and TCP allow the garbled bytes flowing through fiber-optic cables to be routed to their proper destinations and decoded into a meaningful structure. Without protocols, the communication between computers would be random noise, like a Maori and English speaker attempting to hold a conversation.

The Ethereum protocol allows nodes on the Ethereum network to hold a meaningful conversation with each other. Through this conversation, they can broadcast transactions, synchronize nodes, and form the consensus that underpins the network.

Platforms and frameworks are a little more loosely defined. For our purposes, we distinguish them by saying platforms allow applications to be built on top of them, whereas frameworks are (usually software) structures that make building those applications easier.

Ethereum is a platform. We can build and deploy distributed applications, or dapps, onto the Ethereum blockchain. Truffle, which we will encounter in Chapter 2, is a framework. It makes developing, compiling, and deploying Ethereum dapps easy.

CHAPTER 1

Conceptual Introduction

This chapter provides a high-level overview of the Ethereum blockchain. The blockchain is an ordered series of blocks, each of which is an ordered series of transactions. A transaction runs on the Ethereum Virtual Machine and executes code that modifies the state tree. We will explore each of these concepts in more detail in the following sections.

Blocks

As stated previously, a *blockchain* consists of an ordered series of blocks. A *block* consists of a header with meta information and a series of transactions. Blocks are created by miners through the mining process and broadcast to the remainder of the network. Every node verifies received blocks against a series of consensus rules. Blocks that don't satisfy the consensus rules will be rejected by the network.

A *fork* occurs when a network has competing sets of consensus rules. This usually occurs through an update in the official client, which in Ethereum's case is a program called *geth*.

Soft forks occur when the newer set of rules is a subset of the old rules. Clients still using the old rules will not reject blocks created by clients using the new rules, so only block creators (miners) have to update their software.

© Kedar Iyer and Chris Dannen 2018
K. Iyer and C. Dannen, *Building Games with Ethereum Smart Contracts*,
https://doi.org/10.1007/978-1-4842-3492-1_1

Hard forks occur when the new set of rules is incompatible with the old set. In this case, all clients must update their software. Hard forks tend to be contentious. If a group of users refuses to update their software, a *chain split* occurs, and blocks that are valid on one chain will not be valid on the other. There have been six hard forks in Ethereum, one of which led to a chain split and the creation of Ethereum Classic (ETC).

Mining

Mining nodes in the Ethereum network compete to create blocks by using a proprietary proof-of-work algorithm called *Ethash*. The input to the Ethash algorithm is the block header, which includes a randomly generated number called a *nonce*. The output is a 32-byte hex number. Modifying the nonce modifies the output, but in an unpredictable fashion.

For the network to accept a mined block, the Ethash output for the block header must be less than the *network difficulty*, another 32-byte hex number that acts as a target to be beaten. Any miner who broadcasts a block that beats the target difficulty receives a *block reward*. The block reward is awarded by including a *coinbase* transaction in the block. The coinbase transaction is usually the first transaction in the block and sends the block reward to the miner. The current block reward since the Byzantium hard fork is 3 ether.

Sometimes two miners produce a block around the same time, and only one gets accepted into the main chain. The unaccepted block is called an *uncle block*. Uncle blocks are included in the chain and receive a lesser block reward, but their transactions don't modify the state tree.

The security of a blockchain is proportional to the amount of *hashpower* in the network. More hashpower in the network means each individual miner has a smaller percentage of the total hashpower and makes network takeover attacks more difficult (see "51% Attacks" in Chapter 6). Including uncle blocks in the chain increases the security of the chain because the hashpower used to create the unaccepted block doesn't get wasted.

The network difficulty is constantly adjusted so that a block is produced every 15–30 seconds.

Transactions

A *transaction* sends ether, deploys a smart contract, or executes a function on an existing smart contract. Transactions consume *gas*, an Ethereum measurement unit that determines the complexity and network cost of a code operation. The gas cost of a transaction is used to calculate the *transaction fee*. The transaction fee is paid by the address sending the transaction to the miner who mines the block.

Transactions can contain an optional data field. For contract deployment transactions, data is the bytecode of the contract. For transactions sent to a smart contract, data contains the name and arguments for the function to invoke.

Ethereum Virtual Machine (EVM)

A *processor* is an integrated circuit that executes a series of given instructions. Each processor has a set of operations it can perform. An *instruction* consists of an operation code, or *opcode*, followed by input data for the operation. The x86 instruction set is the most common instruction set in use today and has about 1,000 unique opcodes.

A *program* is a set of instructions executing blindly in order. All code—be it punchcards, assembly, or a high-level language such as Python—gets compiled or interpreted down to a series of raw bytes. These bytes correspond to a series of processor instructions that the computer can run in order, like a dumb machine. Listing 1-1 shows what a Hello World program looks like in x86 Linux Assembly.

Listing 1-1. Hello World in x86 Linux Assembly[1]

```
section       .text
global        _start          ;must be declared for linker (ld)

_start:                       ;tell linker entry point

       mov    edx,len         ;message length
       mov    ecx,msg         ;message to write
       mov    ebx,1           ;file descriptor (stdout)
       mov    eax,4           ;system call number (sys_write)
       int    0x80            ;call kernel

       mov    eax,1           ;system call number (sys_exit)
       int    0x80            ;call kernel

section       .data

msg    db    'Hello, world!',0xa    ;our dear string
len    equ $ - msg           ;length of our dear string
```

A *virtual machine*, or VM, is a software program that pretends to be a processor. It has its own set of opcodes and can execute a program tailored specifically to its instruction set. The low-level bytes that correspond to VM instructions are referred to as *bytecode*. Programming languages can be written that compile down to bytecode for execution. The Java Virtual Machine (JVM) is the most popular virtual machine in use today. Some of you make a living off it. It supports multiple languages including Java, Scala, Groovy, and Jython.

Because it is an emulation, a virtual machine has the advantage of being agnostic to the hardware it runs on. Once a virtual machine has been ported to a new platform such as Windows, Linux, or the embedded OS

---

[1]Sourceforge, "Hello World!", http://asm.sourceforge.net/intro/hello.html

in your "smart" refrigerator, programs written for that virtual machine can run equally well on the fridge as on your "smart" TV. Java's "Write Once, Run Anywhere" motto comes to mind.

Ethereum has a VM of its own called the *Ethereum Virtual Machine* (EVM). Ethereum requires its own VM because each opcode in the EVM has an associated gas fee. Fees act as a spam deterrent and allow the EVM to function as a permissionless public resource. Each of the EVM's custom opcodes has its own fee, meaning that well-written contracts can be cheaper to execute. For instance, the SSTORE operation stores data into the state tree, which is an expensive operation because the data has to be replicated across the whole network

The sum of the gas fees accumulated by a transaction's bytecode determines the transaction fee.

State Tree

The primary Ethereum database is its *state tree*, which consists of key/value pairs that map Keccak256 hash keys to a 32-byte value. Data structures in Solidity use one or multiple state tree entries to create programming constructs that are more conducive to programming. A *simple data type* is 32 bytes or less and can be stored in one state tree entry. A *complex data type* like an array requires multiple state tree entries. See the "Data Types" section in Chapter 4 for more on Solidity data structures.

Because a Keccak256 hash is 256 bits long, the Ethereum state tree is designed to store up to 2^{256} unique entries. However, after about 2^{80} entries, hash collisions will make the tree fairly unusable. Either way, this is more disk space than currently exists across the world, so developers can assume that unlimited storage exists. Paying for that storage is another issue, as storing data in the state tree consumes a significant amount of gas. Contracts should be written carefully to minimize the number of insertions and updates they make to the state tree.

The state tree is modified and built up by executing transactions. Most transactions will modify the state tree.

The state tree is implemented as a Merkle Patricia trie. Understanding this data structure is not essential for Solidity programming, but if you are interested, the details are documented on GitHub at `https://github.com/ethereum/wiki/wiki/Patricia-Tree`.

Web3 Explained

Many early adopters of blockchain technologies were excited by its potential to usher in a new era of the Internet—Web 3.0. Web 1.0 was the initial phase of the Internet: a platform used mostly for selling goods and posting information. Web 2.0 introduced social networks and collaboration to the Internet. Sites including Facebook, Flickr, and Instagram brought user-created content front and center. Web 3.0 is the hope for a new decentralized Web, where central authorities no longer have the power to conduct censorship or control user data.

DARPA originally designed the Internet to be a decentralized communication network that could not be taken down by attacking any central authority. As the Web became more commercialized in the last 15 years, the degree of centralization has increased as well.

Scoring well on Google's search algorithm has become a must for new sites to gain traffic. Facebook controls a large percentage of user-generated data and content behind its walled garden. Netflix and YouTube combined account for about one-third of Internet traffic. Countries such as China and Turkey take advantage of this by banning sites that do not agree to their censorship rules.

One of the goals of Web 3.0 is to *re-decentralize* the Web so it is harder to censor and control. Ethereum is an exciting platform for Web 3.0 enthusiasts because any application built on top of it is automatically decentralized.

An application on Ethereum is commonly referred to as a *distributed application*, or *dapp*. Unlike traditional Internet applications, they do not need servers for hosting and data storage. The Ethereum network handles all the traditional duties of the server, including authentication, contract data storage, and an API. This means dapps cannot be censored like traditional sites. Censoring a dapp would require blacklisting every node on the Ethereum network—not a trivial task.

The term *Web3* can lead to a bit of confusion among the Ethereum community. Although initially it referred to the idea of Web 3.0, it now also commonly refers to Ethereum's client library, web3.js. We will be using *web3* to refer to the client library in this book.

What's New with Ethereum

As of this writing, the Ethereum development community is largely focused on two initiatives that may be relevant to developers building dapps with this book:

- *Proof-of-stake*: Both Bitcoin and Ethereum's low-transaction throughput make some applications and services impractical at present. At peak, Bitcoin can process 7 transactions per second (TPS); Ethereum tops out around 30. In contrast, Visa and MasterCard boast tens of thousands of TPS at their peaks. In proof-of-stake (PoS), miners are replaced by *validators*. Swapping out the SHA-256 proof-of-work consensus algorithm for a PoS algorithm could greatly reduce block times, helping Ethereum to increase throughput beyond even Visa and MasterCard's limits.

- *Sharding*: Currently, every full archival node on
  the Ethereum network must download the entire
  blockchain, which as of this writing stands at over
  300GB. Options for "light syncing" are available but are
  not long-term solutions. *Sharding* splits the account
  space into subspaces, each with its own validators,
  removing the requirement for the whole network to
  process every transaction. Transaction throughput
  projections for a sharded, PoS-enabled Ethereum
  network reach as high as 2,000 TPS per shard.

Bitcoin vs. Ethereum

Many of you have received your first exposure to cryptocurrencies and blockchains through Bitcoin. Bitcoin was the first cryptocurrency and is still the largest and most used. It enabled users to send and receive money anywhere in the world without going through a third-party intermediary such as a bank or PayPal. Think of it as counterfeit-proof money for the Internet.

Ethereum's primary innovation over Bitcoin is that it adds a trusted compute framework on top of a blockchain. Ethereum nodes may not necessarily trust each other, but they can trust that the network will execute smart contract code in a deterministic fashion. Combined with the inclusion of a native currency, this allows for a variety of functionality that Bitcoin does not support.

With the exception of hash-locked time contracts, Bitcoin does not support conditional paths. Money is either sent or not sent; the transaction does not depend on the internal state of the system. This may seem trivial, but adding support for conditional paths allows developers *flow of control*, or the ability to specify the order in which individual statements in their program are evaluated and/or executed. An escrow payment is an example of an exchange that is conditional on both parties' participation. Bets are another example of payouts conditional on an external event. Users don't need to trust each other to trust that the smart contract logic will execute as intended.

In many ways, Ethereum is a leap into the unknown. Bitcoin was built to solve the specific problem of creating a decentralized currency. Ethereum offers programmable value transfer based on arbitrary logic, making it conducive to unimagined blockchain-related solutions of the future. The largest use-case at the moment is crowdfunding, but experiments and applications for betting, escrows, decentralized exchanges, prediction markets, decentralized encyclopedias, user-controlled smart data, and more are underway.

Addresses and Keypairs

Ethereum uses the same *asymmetric key cryptography* methods as Bitcoin to authenticate and secure transactions. Public-private keypairs are generated, and messages signed by the *private key* can be decoded only with the corresponding *public key*, and vice versa. An Ethereum *address* is the last 20 bytes of the Keccak256 hash of a public key. Keccak256 is the standard hash function used by Ethereum.

Ether balances tied to an address can be spent by whichever user can prove ownership of the corresponding private key. To do so, all Ethereum transactions are encrypted with the sender's private key. If the user's public key can be used to decrypt the broadcasted message into a valid transaction, that is proof that the user owns the private key.

Contracts and External Accounts

Ethereum has two types of accounts: external accounts and contracts. *External accounts* are controlled by users, whereas *contracts* are semiautonomous entities on the blockchain that can be triggered by a function call. All accounts have an associated balance and nonce. The nonce is incremented after every transaction and exists to prevent duplicate transactions. In addition to these two fields, contracts have access to storage space where they can store additional data fields as specified in their contract code.

Programs in Ethereum

Programs in Ethereum consist of one or more interacting smart contracts. Smart contracts can call functions in other smart contracts. Individual contracts are similar to classes in a traditional language.

Smart contracts can be written in EVM Assembly, Solidity, Low-Level Lisp (LLL), or Serpent. All contracts are eventually compiled down to EVM Assembly bytecode. Solidity is the most commonly used language and the one we will be using. Serpent has been phased out, and LLL usage is rare. New, experimental languages such as Viper are also under development.

Smart contracts are deployed by sending a transaction to the null address (0x0...) with the bytecode as the data.

When Ethereum was designed, its creators envisioned that smart contracts would call upon existing contracts for most of their functionality, with each new smart contract acting as a building block for new contracts on the chain. For example, a contract that wishes to manipulate strings would call on an existing `StringUtils` contract to perform operations like string concatenation that are not supported by Solidity.

Unfortunately, developing in this style requires interacting directly with the Ethereum mainnet for testing and development, which has turned out to be quite expensive. Instead, most developers nowadays would copy a standard `StringUtils` contract into their program so that it's available on a private test chain, and then deploy their own copy of the `StringUtils` contract to use in their program. We will see more examples of this in the game projects in the latter half of the book.

Smart contracts automatically expose an *application binary interface* (ABI), which is the binary or bytecode equivalent of an API. The ABI contains all public and external functions and excludes private and internal functions. ABI functions can be called by either an external account while sending a transaction or by another smart contract while executing its internal logic.

Digging into Solidity

Solidity is the primary programming language for the EVM. Because the EVM has custom `opcodes` that are not used by conventional processors, existing programming languages are an awkward fit for the EVM. Solidity was designed specifically for the task of programming smart contracts on Ethereum.

Solidity receives many comparisons to JavaScript, but its closest relative is C. Solidity is a strongly typed language with minimal functionality that emphasizes limiting storage and CPU usage. It supports 256-bit data types for the EVM, unlike most languages, which support only 32- and 64-bit processors.

Developers who have never worked with a strongly typed language should not find it difficult to adjust to Solidity. Many people actually find typed languages easier to deal with than untyped languages, so don't let that intimidate you. Mobile developers coming from Java, Swift, or Objective-C will find Solidity syntax pretty familiar. JavaScript developers may require some adaptation, as expressions evaluate more easily in loosely typed languages but introduce undesired (and potentially expensive) ambiguities into a system where computation is fee-based.

In a production setting, all developers will have to adjust to working within the gas constraints that limit storage, memory, and CPU usage. Embedded systems developers used to working with limited resources will likely have the easiest transition to Solidity.

Chapter 4 has much more on the ins and outs of working with Solidity.

Staying Hack-Free

Because smart contracts can maintain an ether balance, they are lucrative targets for hackers. Hacks including the DAO attack and Parity multi-sig attack have led to millions of dollars in losses. Most Solidity application code is open source, so following best practices is essential to avoid leaving glaring security flaws in your contract code. These range from interaction techniques such as using a withdrawal method instead of sending ether within a contract (see "Withdrawal Methods" in Chapter 5) to code techniques such as minimizing conditional paths.

In general, Solidity development should be treated more like building a bridge than building a web site. The process is not iterative. Once deployed, a contract's code and ABI cannot be updated. Transferring balances from one contract to another, especially for contracts that maintain an internal ledger, ranges from difficult to impossible.

Whenever possible, proven legacy code should be used instead of new, untested code. Contracts should be thoroughly tested and vetted before being deployed to the mainnet.

Chapter 5 covers contract security in extensive detail. It is the most important chapter in the book. Make sure to read it before attempting to store any assets or ether on a deployed smart contract.

Block Explorers

Block explorers are web sites that provide an easy-to-use interface for navigating a blockchain. Etherscan (`https://etherscan.io/`) is currently the best block explorer available for Ethereum (Figure 1-1). We can use it to check the height of the latest block while syncing, monitor a pending transaction, view the final gas fee for a transaction, check the network difficulty, view the source code or ABI for a deployed contract, and more.

Figure 1-1. *Etherscan block explorer*

We will be using Etherscan extensively in this book to monitor our transactions and wallets. You can search for individual transactions and addresses by using the search box in the upper-right corner.

Useful Smart Contracts

Smart contracts and dapps on the blockchain are an emerging technology, so no prediction about the use of the technology can be made with 100 percent certainty. That being said, many use cases are being explored that look like they have strong potential.

The most proven use case for smart contracts so far is custom tokens and crowdsales. Hundreds of tokens have been launched and sold on Ethereum so far. The crowdsales are usually referred to as *token sales*, initial coin offerings, or ICOs.

Escrow smart contracts have become popular for the transfer of tokens between untrusted parties. The seller grants control of the tokens to the smart contract, and the tokens are sent to the buyer only when the buyer sends ether to the contract.

Other digital assets besides tokens can be stored using smart contracts as well. Companies have built contracts to make stocks, real estate, gold, the US dollar, and many other assets available and tradable on the Ethereum blockchain.

Pros and Cons of Ethereum Gaming

Finally, we arrive at games. Today, game developers have a hard time handling payments, especially in web-hosted games. Gaming sites take deposits and withdrawals from conventional payment frameworks provided by Stripe or PayPal, which often require a few days to clear. Ethereum allows the game logic to integrate payments and micropayments easily.

Using open source smart contracts for games allows for a transparent, reliable method of executing game logic. Historically, users who give their money to sites take on *counterparty risk*, the risk that the owners of the site will never return them the money they are owed. When the FBI shut down a series of poker sites in 2011, many users lost the money they had stored on those sites. Smart contracts on Ethereum can't be shut down or censored. As long as the contract enables users to withdraw ether, they will be able to do so. Properly written smart contracts reduce or eliminate counterparty risk.

Gambling sites are notorious for rigging games of chance—for instance, a digital slot machine that pays out at a lower percentage than advertised. A gambling smart contract with open source code can operate with proven odds, making it *provably fair*.

Gaming on Ethereum has drawbacks. Blocks take 15–30 seconds to propagate, which means that any update to the smart contract such as a bet placement will take 15–30 seconds to propagate. During this pending period before a transaction enters a mined block, that transaction is visible to all participants in the network. Transactions are processed in order of gas price, not time of arrival, so transactions can be front-run by someone paying a higher gas price. If the transaction is the answer to a prize puzzle, an order on an exchange, or anything where secrecy matters, this can cause issues.

People to Follow

Twitter and Reddit are the primary modes of communication in the crypto community. Almost every project has its own public subreddit for community discussion, while general crypto discussions take place on Twitter. Here's a list of tweeters and influencers you can follow to stay up-to-date on all things Ethereum:

- *Vitalik Buterin* (@VitalikButerin): A cofounder of Ethereum and the boy-child wonder genius behind Ethereum. His blog (https://vitalik.ca/) is an absolute must-read for gaining a deeper understanding of blockchain tech.

- *Gavin Wood* (@gavofyork): A cofounder of Ethereum, the creator of Solidity, the writer of the Ethereum yellow paper, and current head of Parity Technologies.

- *Alex Van de Sande* (@avsa): Ethereum Foundation member and head of the Mist Browser team.

- *Vlad Zamfir* (@VladZamfir): One of the primary developers for the Ethereum protocol. Currently working on Casper, Ethereum's next-generation proof-of-stake consensus system.

- *Taylor Gerring* (@TaylorGerring): Helped set up the Ethereum Foundation and used to sit on the Ethereum board.

- *Anthony Diiorio* (@diiorioanthony): Former Ethereum team member and founder of the Jaxx wallet, one of the first wallet apps.

- *Jeffery Wilcke* (@jeffehh): Lead developer of Go Ethereum (geth), the reference client implementation for the Ethereum protocol and EVM.

- *Joe Lubin* (@ethereumJoseph): Ethereum cofounder and founder of ConsenSys, an Ethereum think tank, startup accelerator, code contributor, and more. ConsenSys is one of the largest companies in the Ethereum space.

- *Charles Hoskinson* (@IOHK_Charles): A one-time CEO of Ethereum, he is heavily involved in Ethereum Classic and runs IOHK, a blockchain research company.

Summary

Ethereum is a decentralized compute framework that provides reliable code execution. It is sometimes referred to as the "world computer," and it has the eventual goal of becoming just that. Code on the blockchain is triggered by transactions or internal messages. Transactions are included in blocks and added to the blockchain by miners who secure the chain with their hashpower.

Solidity is the most popular language for creating Ethereum smart contracts. Solidity compiles down to bytecode executing on the Ethereum Virtual Machine (EVM). Each opcode in the EVM has an associated gas fee. Summing the opcode gas fees gives the gas fee for the transaction. Multiplying the gas fee by the user's chosen gas price yields the transaction fee. Miners prioritize transactions by their gas price.

Users secure their ether and on-chain assets with a private key. Any on-chain asset transfer requires the owner of the asset to sign the transaction with their key.

Security is of paramount importance in Ethereum. Hacks caused by poorly written code have led to millions of dollars of value being lost in minutes. We place a heavy emphasis on contract security in this book. Having covered the conceptual basics, you are now ready to write your first smart contracts.

CHAPTER 2

The Ethereum Development Environment

This chapter walks you through the setup and installation of tools required to run the Ethereum blockchain. We cover hardware requirements, operating system requirements, and software requirements. After covering the installation of the software, we provide the basic commands required to interact with the Ethereum network.

Getting Set Up

Coders who have set up a development environment for a compiled language in the past will find the setup for Solidity to be a similar process. Setting up Solidity and the associated tools requires some knowledge of the command line and a UNIX-derived operating system. For first-time developers or those with no command-line experience, we recommend going through the Learn Enough Command Line to Be Dangerous online tutorial (`www.learnenough.com/command-line-tutorial`) before tackling Solidity.

© Kedar Iyer and Chris Dannen 2018
K. Iyer and C. Dannen, *Building Games with Ethereum Smart Contracts*,
https://doi.org/10.1007/978-1-4842-3492-1_2

Hardware Choices

The primary hardware requirements for any blockchain development, not just Ethereum, are a reliable Internet connection and large hard drive.

Syncing a copy of the blockchain with a good Internet connection can take up to 8 hours, though this operation has to be completed only once. Just for the one-time sync, it is recommended to find a minimum 5Mbps download connection to connect to for a night. Syncing on a slower connection, while possible, will simply take longer. Broadcasting transactions, communicating with peers, and downloading new block information all require an always-on, but not necessarily high-bandwidth Internet connection. A connection of 1Mbps download and 512kbps upload should be sufficient for day-to-day operation.

The Ethereum blockchain is large and continually expanding. Running a full archive node, as of December 2017, takes 350GB of disk space.[1] Thankfully, we can run a full node with just the latest snapshot of the state tree, which as of December 2017 occupies only 35GB of disk space. Maintaining the state tree snapshot after syncing requires the equivalent of syncing an archive node from the current block forward. Ideally, you would have 400GB available, but 75GB is the bare minimum you would need available to run a full node.

In addition to the hard disk size, your hard disk must be a solid-state drive (SSD). Using a traditional seeking disk drive (HDD) will be too slow. Any computer manufactured since 2010 will have sufficient compute power and RAM, so those should not be an issue.

---

[1]"Ethereum Database Size", http://bc.daniel.net.nz/

Operating System

All the terminal (command-line) commands in this book are geared toward users on UNIX-derived operating systems. In modern speak, that means if you are running Mac or Linux, you should be fine. Windows users will not find this book difficult to follow, as most of the commands and code are the same across all systems, but should you choose to use Windows, you will be on your own for the installations in the remainder of this section.

Tip   To make following along with the book easier, Windows users can install GNU on Windows, a series of UNIX shell utilities ported over to Windows. The installer can be downloaded from `https://github.com/bmatzelle/gow/wiki`.

Linux

All variants of Linux (Ubuntu, Debian, Red Hat, Arch Linux) already have the necessary tools required to run an Ethereum client. We will be spending a lot of time operating in the command-line interface (CLI). All Linux systems have a built-in CLI program with a name like Terminal, Bash, or Shell. Some variants of Linux are CLI-only. Most aren't. In many Linux systems, the shortcut to access the terminal is Ctrl+Alt+T.

In this book, installation instructions for the required CLI programs are included for both the apt and yum package managers. Package managers make it easy to install other programs and dependencies from the command line. Most Linux distributions come with either apt or yum built in. If you are not sure about which one you have, type both commands into your CLI and see which one works. Figure 2-1 shows the output of the built-in apt manager on Ubuntu.

```
kedar@kedar-Latitude-E6430:~$ apt
apt 1.2.15 (amd64)
Usage: apt [options] command

apt is a commandline package manager and provides commands for
searching and managing as well as querying information about packages.
It provides the same functionality as the specialized APT tools,
like apt-get and apt-cache, but enables options more suitable for
interactive use by default.

Most used commands:
  list - list packages based on package names
  search - search in package descriptions
  show - show package details
  install - install packages
  remove - remove packages
  autoremove - Remove automatically all unused packages
  update - update list of available packages
  upgrade - upgrade the system by installing/upgrading packages
  full-upgrade - upgrade the system by removing/installing/upgrading packages
  edit-sources - edit the source information file

See apt(8) for more information about the available commands.
Configuration options and syntax is detailed in apt.conf(5).
Information about how to configure sources can be found in sources.list(5).
Package and version choices can be expressed via apt_preferences(5).
Security details are available in apt-secure(8).
                                   This APT has Super Cow Powers.
kedar@kedar-Latitude-E6430:~$ █
```

Figure 2-1. *An Ubuntu CLI with apt installed*

If you are a Windows user and would like to try Linux for this book, your first hurdle is getting a Linux distribution installed on your computer. Many detailed tutorials on the Internet indicate how to do so, so we don't cover that here. If you choose to go this route, we recommend using Ubuntu 16.04 LTS with VirtualBox. Ubuntu is the most beginner-friendly version of Linux, and VirtualBox allows you to run a virtual version of Linux without the pain and hassle of partitioning your hard drive and setting up a dual boot.

macOS

Under the hood, macOS and Linux are similar operating systems. Both are descended from UNIX, an operating system developed by Bell Labs in the 1970s. The built-in CLI program in macOS is called *Terminal*, and it has many of the same commands as its Linux counterpart.

> **Note**   Mac, or Macintosh, is the name of the computer produced by Apple, and macOS is the operating system that runs on a Mac. Because the two are always sold together, their names are often used interchangeably.

For our purposes, the key difference between the two CLI environments is the lack of a package manager for macOS. Let's fix that by installing Homebrew. Open the Terminal (you should be able to open it from the Spotlight search pop-up, which can be opened with the shortcut Command+spacebar) and copy in the following command and then press Enter to run the installation:

```
/usr/bin/ruby -e "$(curl -fsSL https://raw.\
githubusercontent.com/Homebrew/install/master/install)"
```

When the installation is complete, type brew into Terminal. You should see a list of available commands.

Programmer's Toolkit

A few basic programming tools are required for any programming project: text editor, compiler/runtime, version control. Let's get these installed before we dive into Ethereum clients.

Text Editor

A *text editor* is a tool for editing plain text. *Plain text* is a format enabling every letter or symbol to be encoded directly into binary. Code and CLIs operate in plain text because it is the simplest compromise between humans who like pretty things and computers that want everything as 0s and 1s. Most word processors do not actually edit plain text. Microsoft Word uses a proprietary format to allow for advanced styling and formatting and because Microsoft likes making it difficult for users to leave its platform.

23

Any standard text editor will be good enough for Solidity development. For those who haven't used a text editor before, Sublime Text or Atom will be a good start. For the Java-heads and mobile developers used to an integrated development environment (IDE), there is an IDE for Ethereum development called Remix, but it has limited functionality and most developers don't use it.

Version Control: git

Version control is an essential tool used to back up code, efficiently track changes in a codebase, and enable clean collaboration between multiple developers. Git is the most popular version control system (VCS). Originally developed by Linus Torvalds to manage the Linux kernel source code, git is now used by the vast majority of software projects.

Note   We will be using git to connect with this book's official GitHub repository at `https://github.com/k26dr/ethereum-games`. The official GitHub repo contains all the project code and links for this book, and will be updated regularly as the Ethereum ecosystem evolves.

Follow Listing 2-1 to install git.

Listing 2-1. Installing git

```
// macOS
brew install git

// Linux
sudo apt-get install git
```

Runtime: JavaScript

The official client library for interacting with an Ethereum node via RPC is web3.js. To use it, we need to install Node.js and NPM. Imagine you dug through the Chrome browser source code, pulled out just the JavaScript engine, and turned it into a command-line program. That's how Ryan Dahl created Node.js, JavaScript's server-side sister. Node.js uses a module system to organize code, similar to Java or Python or Swift. NPM, Node.js Package Manager, was created to streamline this process and make sharing modules via the Web easy. Think of it as apt or yum for Node.js modules. To install, follow Listing 2-2.

Listing 2-2. Installing Node.js and NPM

```
// macOS
brew install node

// Linux w/ apt
// The second line creates a shortcut from the node command
// to the nodejs program for consistency with the macOS
// package name
sudo apt-get install nodejs npm
sudo ln -s /usr/bin/nodejs /usr/bin/node
```

Compiler: Solidity

Solidity is a compiled language that compiles into EVM bytecode similar to Java. The Solidity compiler will be the first NPM package we install. Install it globally with the following:

```
sudo npm install -g solc
```

Ethereum Clients

The *Ethereum client* is the program that implements the Ethereum protocol and interacts with the Ethereum network and blockchain. Here are some of its responsibilities:

- Sync new chains

- Download and verify new blocks

- Connect to peers

- Verify and execute transactions

- Broadcast local transactions to the network

- Provide basic mining ability

There are multiple Ethereum clients, each with its own pros and cons. We will be using two in this book, geth and TestRPC, but cover two more, Eth and Parity, so you can be familiar with them.

Geth

Geth is the official Go implementation of the Ethereum protocol. It is the most up-to-date Ethereum client and serves as the reference client for all Ethereum updates. As the official reference implementation for Ethereum, geth has all the latest security patches and updates. To install geth, follow Listing 2-3.

Listing 2-3. Installing geth

```
# This is a comment
# Any lines starting with '#' will be ignored by the CLI

# For Linux w/ apt
sudo apt-get install software-properties-common
```

```
sudo add-apt-repository -y ppa:ethereum/ethereum
sudo apt-get update
sudo apt-get install ethereum
# For Mac
brew tap ethereum/ethereum
brew install ethereum
```

TestRPC

TestRPC is a lightweight Ethereum client that specializes in running private chains for development. We will use it to create private networks that are sandboxed from the mainnet. It is built into the Truffle framework, and we cover it along with Truffle later in this chapter.

Eth

Eth is the official C++ implementation of the Ethereum protocol. It is used in applications such as mining that require high performance. It used to support the mining algorithm itself, but that portion of the codebase has since been spun off into its own project called *Ethminer*.

Parity

Parity is a third-party Ethereum client that aims to provide a user-friendly alternative to the geth client and Mist browser. Its development is led by Gavin Wood, an Ethereum cofounder and a prominent member of the community. Parity is targeted at Ethereum users rather than developers and tends to lag geth in having the latest features.

Deployment

Ethereum has two types of addresses: wallet addresses and contract addresses. They look and act the same, but one belongs to a user, and one belongs to a contract. Only the owner of the private key can send the ether belonging to a wallet address. A contract address can have a balance, just like a wallet address. Only the contract code can send the ether belonging to the contract.

Creating a contract is simple in theory; send the contract bytecode to the null address (0x). In practice, though, going from a Solidity contract to EVM bytecode with a hand-rolled process is a messy affair, so we're going to pull in one more dependency to simplify the process.

Introducing Truffle

Truffle is a development framework for Solidity and the EVM. Truffle will take care of compiling, deploying, and testing our contracts and allow us to focus on writing the game contracts. To install Truffle globally, use this command:

```
sudo npm install -g truffle
```

Let's get a feel for Truffle by running some basic commands. We will go more into the theory of how all this works later. For now, we're going to deploy our first contract to a private chain. Run the commands in Listing 2-4 in the order provided. The truffle develop command will open a Truffle development console running TestRPC. The migrate command should be run in that console.

Tip Windows users should use truffle.cmd instead of truffle for Truffle commands. As an example, truffle.cmd develop would open the Truffle dev console.

Listing 2-4. Deploying a sample dapp with Truffle

```
mkdir truffle-test
cd truffle-test
truffle init
truffle develop

# Run this command in the Truffle dev console
migrate

# Exit the dev console
.exit
```

truffle init scaffolds a series of folders and sample files, one of which is the contracts folder. You should see a Solidity contract file in there: Migrations.sol. Take a quick browse through the code in the file. That is the code we just deployed, and reading through it will give you a feel for how Solidity contracts are structured.

Migrating is the Truffle equivalent of deploying. A migration in Truffle is essentially a deployment script. One of the directories scaffolded by Truffle is the migrations/ folder. There should be a sample migration file in there as well. Take a look at it to see what a simple migration looks like.

Congratulations! You've set up a development chain for yourself and deployed your first Solidity contract.

Basic Geth Commands

Geth is an in-depth program that handles a large deal of functionality. Run geth help to see a full list of commands available in geth. It is quite comprehensive. We're going to focus on a small subset of essential commands in this section.

The first command we're going to try out is no command. Run geth with no options or commands. You should see something similar to Figure 2-2. Geth is starting up for the first time, connecting to peers, and beginning the sync process. Use Ctrl+C to exit geth.

```
kedar@kedar-Latitude-E6430:~$ geth
INFO [09-28|14:16:00] Starting peer-to-peer node               instance=Geth/v1.6.7-stable-ab5646c5/linux-amd64/go1.8.1
INFO [09-28|14:16:00] Allocated cache and file handles         database=/home/kedar/.ethereum/geth/chaindata cache=128 han
INFO [09-28|14:16:00] Initialised chain configuration          config="{ChainID: 1 Homestead: 1150000 DAO: 1920000 DAOSupp
000 Metropolis: 9223372036854775807 Engine: ethash}"
INFO [09-28|14:16:00] Disk storage enabled for ethash caches   dir=/home/kedar/.ethereum/geth/ethash count=3
INFO [09-28|14:16:00] Disk storage enabled for ethash DAGs     dir=/home/kedar/.ethash           count=2
INFO [09-28|14:16:00] Initialising Ethereum protocol           versions="[63 62]" network=1
INFO [09-28|14:16:00] Loaded most recent local header          number=4256707 hash=e61711..410d6d td=89117296270707611076
INFO [09-28|14:16:00] Loaded most recent local full block      number=4256707 hash=e61711..410d6d td=89117296270707611076
INFO [09-28|14:16:00] Loaded most recent local fast block      number=4256707 hash=e61711..410d6d td=89117296270707611076
WARN [09-28|14:16:00] Blockchain not empty, fast sync disabled
INFO [09-28|14:16:00] Starting P2P networking
INFO [09-28|14:16:02] UDP listener up                          self=enode://4d6897fab3e0de4a67cf8e1126a1245a2cf80331003c62
825d7775276a26a0b3b62f80844a0[::]:30303
INFO [09-28|14:16:02] RLPx listener up                         self=enode://4d6897fab3e0de4a67cf8e1126a1245a2cf80331003c62
825d7775276a26a0b3b62f80844a0[::]:30303
INFO [09-28|14:16:02] IPC endpoint opened: /home/kedar/.ethereum/geth.ipc
INFO [09-28|14:16:22] Block synchronisation started
```

Figure 2-2. *Geth on startup*

To interact with geth, we need to open geth in console mode. Let's do so with the command geth console. You should see something like Figure 2-3 pop up.

```
kedar@kedar-Latitude-E6430:~$ geth --verbosity 0 console
Welcome to the Geth JavaScript console!

instance: Geth/v1.6.7-stable-ab5646c5/linux-amd64/go1.8.1
coinbase: 0xf2e6b44e0ffd524bd36cae1a58d9f6ee2edffb1e
at block: 4256707 (Sat, 09 Sep 2017 18:27:32 EDT)
 datadir: /home/kedar/.ethereum
 modules: admin:1.0 debug:1.0 eth:1.0 miner:1.0 net:1.0 personal:1.0

> web3.eth.accounts
```

Figure 2-3. *Geth console*

The geth console exposes a series of modules that allow us to interact with geth. This includes functionality for creating wallets, sending ether, creating contracts, interacting with contracts, and more. As an example, to view a list of our wallets, we could input eth.accounts into the console.

We don't have any wallets generated at the moment, so we receive back an empty array. We will be generating wallets and obtaining ether in Project 3-1, and we will revisit the geth console and its many commands at that time. Type `exit` in the console to quit the program.

Many users find the log messages flowing across the geth console to be distracting. To silence the log messages, run the console in silent mode with `geth --verbosity 0 console`.

In addition to the mainnet, geth can be used to access testnets, run private nets, and interact with any other network that observes the Ethereum protocol. We will regularly be connecting to the Rinkeby testnet in this book to test and deploy contracts without having to use any of our precious ether. To connect to the Rinkeby testnet, run `geth --rinkeby`. This will connect to Rinkeby peers and begin the sync process for the Rinkeby network.

Account and wallet management is one of the core features of geth, especially for nondevelopers. To access the account management interface, run `geth account`. This will pull up a help page and list of subcommands that can be used for account management. Let's test one of the commands right now by running `geth account list`. Just as in the console section, you will receive an empty response. The command `geth account new` can be used to create a new account, but we will hold off on doing so until later in the chapter.

To communicate with dapps and external clients, geth can run a JSON-RPC server. To run geth in RPC mode, use `geth --rpc`. For security reasons, RPC mode by default disables access to local private keys. We will be needing RPC access to our private keys to sign and send transactions, so we will run the RPC server with `geth --rpc --rpcapi web3,eth,net,personal`. The personal module enables access to account services.

Caution   Enabling the personal RPC API exposes your geth wallets to the Internet. The only thing preventing others from stealing your ether will be your wallet password. Make sure it is strong. We will be repeating this warning multiple times throughout the book.

Sometimes we will want to run two networks at the same time. Later in the chapter, we will be doing this to sync both the mainnet and Rinkeby testnet at the same time. By default, geth connects to port 30303 for network actions and 8545 for the RPC server. Only one program can be listening on a port at a time, so attempting to run two instances of geth at the same time will fail by default. To have one of the instances listen on a different network port (say, 31303), run geth `--port 31303`. To have one of the RPC servers run on a different port (say, 9545), run geth `--rpc --rpcport 9545`.

Docs and Resources

The geth docs can be found on GitHub at `https://github.com/ethereum/go-ethereum/wiki/geth` The page has links to both the geth console API and geth command reference.

Table 2-1 is a reference for useful geth commands. Some are covered in this chapter, and others are not covered until later chapters but are included here for completeness.

Table 2-1. *Useful Geth Commands*

Description	Command
Default geth mode, used for basic operation	`geth`
Interactive console (silent mode)	`geth console --verbosity 0`
Command reference	`geth help`
Rinkeby testnet	`geth --rinkeby`
Account management	`geth account`
Create account	`geth account new`
Sync mainnet	`geth --fast --cache=1024`
Sync Rinkeby	`geth --rinkeby --fast --cache=1024`
RPC mode	`geth --rpc`
RPC mode with local wallet access	`geth --rpc --rpcapi web3,eth,net,personal`
Listen on custom network port	`geth --port <port>`
Listen on custom RPC port	`geth --rpc --rpcport <port>`

Connecting to the Blockchain

To execute contract deployments and network transactions, you have to sync a full node for each network you wish to use. We will be syncing two networks for this book: the Ethereum main network (mainnet) and the Rinkeby test network (testnet). A *test network* is a network that runs the Ethereum protocol, but whose token has no value. It's useful for testing code, deployments, and transactions without paying gas fees, which can be prohibitively expensive for repetitive testing.

Every public Ethereum network has a unique network ID. The network ID of the Ethereum mainnet is 1. The network ID of the Rinkeby testnet is 4. The network ID of our private chains will be large, random numbers whose only job is to be unique enough to avoid syncing with other networks.

Network Synchronization

Geth offers three modes for network synchronization: light, full, and archive.

A *light node* syncs block headers, but does not process transactions or maintain a state tree. Light clients are useful for users who wish only to maintain wallets and send/receive ether. For developers, a light client will be insufficient; we will require a full node.

A *full node* maintains a local snapshot of the blockchain state tree, downloads full blocks, executes block transactions on its local copy of the blockchain, and participates in the consensus process. Full nodes are the backbone of the Ethereum network. For those of you familiar with torrents, think of the full vs. light client dynamic as analogous to seeds vs. leeches. Full nodes seed network information to peers, whereas light nodes leech information from the network without seeding anything back. Syncing a full node is a slow process that takes about 8 hours and consumes about 30GB of disk space.

An *archive node*, sometimes referred to as a *full archive node*, maintains not only a current snapshot of the state tree, but also a copy of every state transition that has occurred on the chain since the genesis block. A full archive node is the granddaddy of Ethereum nodes, and as of December 2017, consumes 350GB of space while growing at a rate of 30GB per month. If syncing a full node is a slow process, syncing an archive node is damn near impossible. Estimates on my laptop with a standard SSD and 10Mbps Internet connection placed the sync time at 45 days. For those wishing to run an archive node, your best bet is to use geth's import/export functionality to make a copy of the database from an existing archive node.

We will be syncing full nodes for the mainnet and Rinkeby testnet.

Mainnet

To sync a full node on the mainnet, run the following:

```
geth --fast --cache=1024
```

A fast sync will sync a full node without archives. This process takes about 8 hours on a 10Mbps or faster Internet connection with an SSD drive. Using an HDD takes two to three times longer. The same goes for connections below 3Mpbs. Leave the sync running overnight if you can, and you should be ready in the morning. To save time, you can sync both the mainnet and the testnet at the same time. We explain how to do so in the next section.

Testnet

For the testnet, we will be syncing to the Rinkeby testnet. Past testnets for Ethereum include Olympic, Morden, Ropsten, and Kovan. The Kovan testnet is still active but has been mostly supplanted by the Rinkeby testnet. The other testnets have all been abandoned. Maintaining a testnet turns out to be quite a difficult task, and they get successfully attacked quite regularly. More on this can be found in the "Testnet Attacks and Issues" section in Chapter 6.

We assume that most of you will be syncing the testnet at the same time as the mainnet, so we will run the testnet sync on a different port:

```
geth --rinkeby --port 31303
```

Leave both networks to sync overnight, and resume the exercises in this book when the syncs are complete.

Faucets

Mainnet Ether can be purchased on an exchange with bitcoin or fiat currency, but no exchange will list testnet ether because it has no value. To solve this problem, most testnets use faucets. *Faucets* are sites that send you free crypto. They originated in the early bitcoin days as a quick way for users to obtain small amounts of bitcoin to get a feel for the technology, but faded away after the coin gained serious value. Nowadays they are used seriously only for testnets.

Summary

Running an Ethereum node requires a large solid-state hard drive and a good Internet connection. 75GB of SSD disk space and a 5Mpbs connection are an ideal minimum.

The best operating system for developing Ethereum smart contracts is Linux, with macOS a close second. If you must use Windows, make sure to download GNU on Windows and use `truffle.cmd` instead of `truffle` for your Truffle commands.

An Ethereum client takes care of syncing and maintaining a local copy of the blockchain. It allows us to broadcast transactions and interact with deployed contracts. The two main clients we will use are geth and TestRPC. TestRPC provides a local dev chain, and geth allows us to connect to the mainnet and Rinkeby testnet. In the next chapter, we will use the tools and concepts from this chapter to broadcast a simple transaction and deploy our first contract.

CHAPTER 3

First Steps with Ethereum

This chapter is the first of our applied practice chapters. It walks through the two fundamental Ethereum interactions. In the first project, we will broadcast a transaction to three Ethereum networks. In the second project, we will deploy a simple Hello World contract.

Project 3-1: Creating Transactions

In this exercise, we will use the geth console to send ether. You may have used a wallet service to send ether in the past. We will be using JavaScript, the language of the geth console, and web3.js, Ethereum's official client library, to send ether in the command line. If you don't know JavaScript, don't worry. This exercise won't require any complex code.

Generating Wallets

To send ether, we need to own ether. And to own ether, we need a wallet. So let's generate a couple of wallets. Some of you may not be able to obtain ether for the mainnet, so we will conduct the exercise on both the mainnet and the testnet.

© Kedar Iyer and Chris Dannen 2018

K. Iyer and C. Dannen, *Building Games with Ethereum Smart Contracts*,
https://doi.org/10.1007/978-1-4842-3492-1_3

Mainnet

To generate a wallet on the mainnet, run this command:

```
geth account new
```

You should be prompted for a passphrase.

Tip   During the course of this book, we will use "ethereum" as the password for all private keys generated in sample projects and exercises. *Do not* copy this or any other password; choose your own.

Later, when we enable the personal module in geth's RPC server, the only thing standing between you and personal crypto ruin will be that password. Use a strong password.

If you're wondering why nothing is showing up on the screen as you type your password, that's standard practice for the command line; passwords are completely hidden. Enter and confirm your password, and your new address will display.

After the first account is created, create a second account to act as the receiver for the transaction.

Testnet

To create an account on the testnet, run the following:

```
geth --rinkeby account new
```

Create two accounts for the testnet as well.

Obtaining Ether

To send ether, we need to have ether, so let's get ourselves some.

Mainnet

There are two ways to obtain ether: buy it directly with fiat, or buy bitcoin and then purchase ether with bitcoin. Readers in the United States, Canada, and Europe can use Coinbase (`www.coinbase.com`) or Gemini (`https://gemini.com`) to purchase ether from a bank account or credit card. Readers in China can use OKCoin (`www.okcoin.com`) or BTCC (`www.btcc.com`). Readers from any other country can use Coinmama (`www.coinmama.com`) to purchase ether directly from a credit card.

For those without access to a credit card, you have to purchase bitcoin first. LocalBitcoins (`https://localbitcoins.com`) is the best way to purchase bitcoin directly with cash across the world. After you have bitcoin, you can use ShapeShift (`https://shapeshift.io/`) or any of the exchanges mentioned previously to convert your bitcoin into ether.

If you are unable to obtain ether, or the process is taking too long, know that you do not need mainnet ether to do any of the projects in this book. The Rinkeby testnet is the same as the mainnet in every way, aside from the value of the token. The games might not feel as real without real money at play, but the differences will be psychological, not technical.

Testnet

Rinkeby uses a faucet to distribute "test ether" to developers (see `https://faucet.rinkeby.io/`). Ether received from the faucet cannot be used or spent on the mainnet. You can verify that your testnet transactions are successful by entering your account address into the search box on the Rinkeby Etherscan site (`https://rinkeby.etherscan.io/`). The transaction that sent my account 3 test ether is at `https://rinkeby.etherscan.io/tx/0xe51f16a048a3832897b19e3cb5ab861d1d708724c47a7 6d974739604d2bd9b1d`.

After the transaction confirms, open a Rinkeby geth console (geth --rinkeby --verbosity 0 console). Check your balance with this command:

```
eth.getBalance(eth.accounts[0])
```

If you used your second generated address instead of the first one, pass in eth.accounts[1] instead. eth.getBalance(*address*) can be used to check the balance of any address on the network, even ones that don't belong to you.

You should see a big positive number similar to Figure 3-1.

```
> eth.getBalance(eth.accounts[0])
300000000000000000000
```

Figure 3-1. *Wallet balance*

This is your balance in wei, the base unit of ether. There are 10^{18} wei in 1 ether, so view your balance in ether with this command:

```
eth.getBalance(eth.accounts[0]) / 1e18
```

JavaScript recognizes scientific notation, so the number you see is your balance in Rinkeby ether.

Sending Fake Ether with the Geth Command Line

We're ready to make our first transaction! Let's use the Rinkeby testnet to send some of the fake ether you just obtained to the author's address. Open a Rinkeby geth console (don't forget the --rinkeby flag or you will accidentally send real ether) and use web3 to send a transaction (Listing 3-1).

Listing 3-1. Sending Ether

```
eth.sendTransaction({
  from: eth.accounts[0],
  to: "0x2fbd98e03bd62996b68cc90dd874c570a1f94dcc",
  value: 1e17,
  gas: 90e3,
  gasPrice: 20e9
})
```

Hold up! We just got an error: `Error: authentication needed: password or unlock`. It turns out we need to unlock the account before we can use it. To unlock your account:

```
// replace password with the passphrase for the account
personal.unlockAccount(eth.accounts[0], password)
```

Now we can run our send function again. You can use the up and down arrows to scroll through the command history. Rerun the code in Listing 3-1. You should now get back a long hex. That hex is a transaction ID. If you look up the transaction ID on the Rinkeby Etherscan site, you will see the details of your transaction. If you click the account address in the To field (Figure 3-2), you'll be able to see a list of all the other readers who have made the same transaction!

Transaction Information	
TxHash:	0x5cf9afdd1d6b581c52ba3fa7ac332d58549a77be7f8c96fcdc94b2cff7482eb5
Block Height:	1383069 (25 block confirmations)
TimeStamp:	6 mins ago (Dec-09-2017 07:56:08 AM +UTC)
From:	0x0cb510e2f16c36ce039ee3164330d5f00ecf9eac
To:	0x4eac9a8c7a6c3a869cdbff4e06cb552148749206

Figure 3-2. Etherscan "To" field

Let's circle back to the send function and go over the details of our transaction. The proper syntax for the function is `eth.sendTransaction` (*txOptions*). The `tx` is shorthand for *transaction*, an abbreviation you'll see many times in the blockchain world. The *txOptions* object will be a part of every transaction we send using web3.js. It uses a total of seven keys, but the five we used are the ones you will see most often:

- `from`: The sender. This account must be unlocked so it can sign the transaction.

- `to`: The recipient. Leave it blank to send a contract creation transaction to the null address. Optional, but you will never use it to create a contract directly, so it should be set.

- `value`: The amount to send in wei. Optional, defaults to 0.

- `gas`: The maximum amount of gas the transaction can use. Any unused gas is refunded to the user. If the gas limit is exceeded, the transaction will throw an `OutOfGasError` and revert all state changes. Optional, defaults to 90e3.

- `gasPrice`: The price per unit of gas for this transaction in wei. Gas prices are usually discussed in Gwei (10^9 wei). Transactions on the mainnet are prioritized by gas price. Transactions with higher gas prices (~40 Gwei) tend to get mined by the next block. Transactions with low gas prices (~1 Gwei) generally take 5–10 minutes to mine. Optional, defaults to the mean network gas price. The mean network gas price on the mainnet as of December 2017 is about 10 Gwei.

- `data`: The raw bytecode data to send along with the transaction. Web3 has helpers to take care of the details of this for us. Optional; we will rarely use this field.

- nonce: An auto-incrementing counter to signal the uniqueness of a transaction to the network. Setting it manually allows you to override a transaction that hasn't been mined yet. If you set a gas price too low, you can override it with a higher gas price by using the same nonce as in the transaction you want to override. Optional; we will not use it in this book.

The total cost of a transaction is calculated by (gas used) × (gas price). A send operation like the one we executed consumes 21,000 gas. At our specified gas price of 20 Gwei, our operation cost 0.00042 ether. Etherscan is a great resource for checking transaction details. It lists whether your transaction is pending or has been mined, when it was mined, the gas used, and the total transaction cost; and it converts all these numbers to dollars at the current market rate. Figure 3-3 shows a sample transaction receipt on Etherscan.

Overview	Comments
Transaction Information	
TxHash:	0xcb6860d6f9a415e6a26a8b8e44316618b6306aeea5da84ac9e87618a6dade4b0
Block Height:	4273423 (1 block confirmation)
TimeStamp:	37 secs ago (Sep-14-2017 02:55:20 PM +UTC)
From:	0x2a65aca4d5fc5b5c859090a6c34d164135398226 (DwarfPool1)
To:	0xb86a7009b6ec11464b6548a73db63117474a4841
Value:	0.58865008 Ether ($146.39)
Gas Limit:	90000
Gas Used By Txn:	21000
Gas Price:	0.00000002 Ether (20 Gwei)
Actual Tx Cost/Fee:	0.00042 Ether ($0.10)
Cumulative Gas Used:	6627749
Nonce:	2640204

Figure 3-3. *Etherscan transaction receipt*

43

CHALLENGE: SEND ETHER ON THE MAINNET

The process for sending ether on the mainnet is the same as sending ether on the testnet aside from the choice of network on geth. Connect to the mainnet by using geth. Using the two wallets you created earlier, send ether from one wallet to the other and trace the transactions on Etherscan. Vary the gas prices and watch your execution times change.

The challenge here is to slowly increase the values you're sending until you're comfortable sending large amounts of money across the network. As you get deeper into the crypto world, you will find yourself making large transactions in which an error such as mistyping an address or leaving a field blank can send your ether into the void. Gaining the confidence and skill to make large transactions is essential to becoming a crypto master!

Project 3-2: Deployment 101

In this exercise, we're going to deploy our first contract, a simple Hello World contract. We will first deploy the contract manually, walking through the steps required to make that happen, and then use Truffle to make the same deployment and watch the difficulties fade away.

Hello World Contract

Here's the code for our simple Hello World contract. Enter the code in Listing 3-2 into a new file at contracts/HelloWorld.sol. We won't cover the details of the contract in depth until Chapter 4. For now, the goal is to deploy a contract to an Ethereum network.

Listing 3-2. Hello World Contract

```solidity
pragma solidity ^0.4.15;

contract HelloWorld {
    address owner;
    string greeting = "Hello World";

    // Constructor function
    function HelloWorld () public {
        owner = msg.sender;
    }

    function greet () constant public returns (string) {
        return greeting;
    }

    function kill () public {
        require(owner == msg.sender);
        selfdestruct(owner);
    }
}
```

There are three functions in this contract. All three functions are marked as public and can be accessed via the contract ABI.

The first function, the constructor function, has the same name as our contract and executes when the contract is deployed. It sets the contract deployer as the owner of the contract.

The greet function is a constant function, meaning invoking it doesn't modify the state tree or require a network transaction. This is what we will use to display our greeting.

The `kill` function is a common function we will be using in all our contracts. It allows the contract to self-destruct, or remove itself from the state tree to prevent blockchain bloat. Only the owner of the contract can kill the contract. As a good Ethereum citizen, you should be killing all your unused contracts.

Manual Deployment

We're going to manually compile and deploy our contract to the testnet to understand how smart contracts work under the hood. This will be the first and last time we do a manual deployment in this book. In your terminal, `cd` into the `contracts/` folder and then run the following command to compile the contract:

```
solcjs --bin --abi -o bin HelloWorld.sol
```

The `--bin` and `--abi` flags indicate that we want to output bytecode and ABI, respectively. One file will be created for each in our indicated output folder `bin/`.

To deploy this contract, we have to send a transaction to the empty address with the bytecode in the `data` field of the *txObject*. We could write a script to do this for us, but because we will be doing this only once, let's do it manually. Open the bytecode file that was created, `bin/HelloWorld_sol_HelloWorld.bin,` and copy the giant hex in the file into the clipboard. Open the Rinkeby geth console, and store the hex as a string in the variable `bytecode` (Figure 3-4).

```
kedar@kedar-Latitude-E6430:~/code/ethereum-games/contracts$ geth --rinkeby --verbosity 0 console
Welcome to the Geth JavaScript console!

instance: Geth/v1.6.7-stable-ab5646c5/linux-amd64/go1.8.1
coinbase: 0x2fbd98e03bd62996b68cc90dd874c570a1f94dcc
at block: 893374 (Thu, 14 Sep 2017 14:06:17 EDT)
 datadir: /home/kedar/.ethereum/rinkeby
 modules: admin:1.0 clique:1.0 debug:1.0 eth:1.0 miner:1.0 net:1.0 personal:1.0 rpc:1.0 txpool:1.0 web3:1.0

> bytecode = "60606040526040805190810160405280600b81526020017f48656c6c6f6f20576f726c6400000000000000000000000000
341561005b57600080fd5b5b336000806101000a81548173ffffffffffffffffffffffffffffffffffffffff021916908373ffffffff
600116156101000203166002900490600052602060002090601f016020900481019282601f106100e357806101900ff1916838001178555
5591602001919060001019061001f5565b5b50905061011e91906101122565b5090565b61014491905b808211156101401576000816000090
40526000357c0100000000000000000000000000000000000000000000000000000000900463ffffffff16806341c0e1b51461004957
565b005b3415610056000695760008fd5b610071610184565b6040518080602001828103825283818151815181526020019150805190602001900190
505050905090810190601f1680156100df5780820380516001836020003610101000a03191681526020200191505b50925050505060405180
6101000a900473ffffffffffffffffffffffffffffffffffffffffffffffffff1673ffffffffffffffffffffffffffffffffffffffff1614151561
ffffffffffffff1673ffffffffffffffffffffffffffffffffffffffff16ff5b565b61018c61022d565b600180546001816001161561
9081815260200182805460018160011615610100020316600290048015610222257806001106101017576101010008035404028352916020
831161020557829003601f168201915b50505050505090505b90565b6020604051908101604052806000008152509050600a165627a7a72300
0029"
```

Figure 3-4. *Copying bytecode into the geth console*

Now deploy the contract (Listing 3-3). Make sure to replace *password* with your password.

Listing 3-3. Deploy EVM Bytecode Contract

```
// replace password with your password
personal.unlockAccount(eth.accounts[0], password)
tx = eth.sendTransaction({ from: eth.accounts[0], data:
bytecode, gas: 500e3 })
```

Omitting the to field in the address defaults to the empty address. Including a data field in a transaction to the empty address will execute a contract creation transaction. sendTransaction returns a transaction ID. To get the address of the contract that was just deployed, repeatedly attempt to get the transaction receipt as in Figure 3-5. This will return null until the transaction is mined. Expect the transaction to take about 30 seconds to get mined.

```
> tx = eth.sendTransaction({ from: eth.accounts[0],  data: bytecode, gas: 500e3 })
"0x27747e74f090e9045e8e25be8d0be6a7cf7645fd921df861d20cb4dc439a75c0"
> tx
"0x27747e74f090e9045e8e25be8d0be6a7cf7645fd921df861d20cb4dc439a75c0"
> web3.eth.getTransactionReceipt(tx)
null
> web3.eth.getTransactionReceipt(tx)
null
> web3.eth.getTransactionReceipt(tx)
null
> web3.eth.getTransactionReceipt(tx)
null
> web3.eth.getTransactionReceipt(tx)
null
> web3.eth.getTransactionReceipt(tx)
{
  blockHash: "0xd060763c608ba31c9c3d1e54fe607df9b470f24688d99e43930830e67474807f",
  blockNumber:        ,
  contractAddress: "0xed912a558878bb84669d12abc79122fdb165561a",
  cumulativeGasUsed:       ,
  from: "0x2fbd98e03bd62996b68cc90dd874c570a1f94dcc",
  gasUsed:       ,
  logs: [],
  logsBloom: "0x00000000000000000000000000000000000000000000000000000000000000000000
0000000000000000000000000000000000000000000000000000000000000000000000000000000000000000
0000000000000000000000000000000000000000000000000000000000000000000000000000000000000000
",
  root: "0xd2f66992126a24df12559a2681d9845298d6493e653f7063035496d36581c1b4",
  to: null,
  transactionHash: "0x27747e74f090e9045e8e25be8d0be6a7cf7645fd921df861d20cb4dc439a75c0",
  transactionIndex:
}
>
```

Figure 3-5. *Attempting to get a transaction receipt*

To interact with the contract, we need to know the contract's address and ABI. The address can be obtained from the transaction receipt. Get the address with this code:

```
address = web3.eth.getTransactionReceipt(tx).contractAddress
```

The compiler outputs the ABI as one of the compilation outputs, so we need to copy that in just as we did to the bytecode. Copy the contents of the file bin/HelloWorld_sol_HelloWorld.abi and store it in the variable abi. You should get something like Figure 3-6.

```
> abi = [{ "constant": false, "inputs": [], "name": "kill", "outputs": [], "payable": f
alse, "type": "function" }, { "constant": true, "inputs": [], "name": "greet", "outputs
": [ { "name": "", "type": "string" } ], "payable": false, "type": "function" }, { "inp
uts": [], "payable": false, "type": "constructor" }]
```

Figure 3-6. *Hello World contract ABI*

With both of those loaded, we can use web3 to create a contract object and call our greet function:

```
HelloWorld = web3.eth.contract(abi).at(address)
HelloWorld.greet()
```

You should see the greeting "Hello World" pop up in your console. Whew! We did it. We deployed a contract manually without Truffle. Thankfully, we won't be doing that again. Let's do the same deployment with Truffle now.

Deploying with Truffle

Truffle is going to greatly simplify our deployment process. With a little bit of configuration, it will allow us to easily deploy a contract to private chains, the testnet, and the mainnet.

Private Chain

Before we can deploy our contract, Truffle requires us to write a migration file. Remember, migration files are the Truffle equivalent of deployment files.

Create a new file in the `migrations/` folder called `2_hello_world.js` and copy Listing 3-4 into it.

Listing 3-4. Hello World Simple Migration

```
var HelloWorld = artifacts.require("./HelloWorld.sol");

module.exports = function(deployer) {
    deployer.deploy(HelloWorld);
};
```

This is the simplest form of migration we can write. Truffle migrations are required to export a callback that executes when the migration runs. The callback takes the *deployer* as its first argument. We use this deployer to deploy our contract.

Let's run this migration to deploy our contract. As before, the `migrate` command will go inside the console opened by the `develop` command.

Don't exit the console with `exit` this time. We will continue using the dev console to interact with the contract after deploying it.

```
truffle develop
migrate -f 2
```

And voila, we're deployed. So much easier than a manual deployment, isn't it? The `-f` flag forces Truffle to run a specific migration. More about the migration process is explained in Chapter 4.

To interact with the contract, we continue using the dev console. The console automatically loads up our deployed contracts. To run the `greet` function, here is the command:

```
HelloWorld.deployed().then(h => h.greet())
```

For all our contracts, the `.deployed` function will return a promise to the most recently deployed version of the contract. We can then call any of the ABI functions on the returned instance.

Testnet

For the testnet and mainnet, additional Truffle configuration is required. Configuration settings for our Truffle project are contained in the `truffle.js` file in the project root. The project root is the folder where you ran the `truffle init` command. Modify the `truffle.js` file so it looks like Listing 3-5.

Listing 3-5. Truffle Configuration

```
module.exports = {
    networks: {
        development: {
            host: "localhost",
            port: 8545,
            network_id: "*" // Match any network id
        },

        // NEW CONFIGURATION INFO HERE
        rinkeby: {
            host: "localhost",
            port: 8545,
            network_id: 4
        },
        mainnet: {
            host: "localhost",
            port: 8545,
            network_id: 1
        }
    }
};
```

The truffle migrate command has a --network flag that allows you to specify which network configuration you wish to use. By default, the truffle.js file contains only configuration information for a development network. As you'll see soon, the migration script we wrote for TestRPC will have to be modified for geth networks, so we have included two additional networks in the configuration file.

By specifying network IDs for Rinkeby and the mainnet, we can eliminate a common source of user error in deployments. Truffle will verify during every deployment that the expected network ID matches the Ethereum client's network ID. If we try to deploy a script to the testnet with a command such as `truffle migrate --network rinkeby`, but are accidentally running geth on the mainnet, Truffle will reject the deployment.

Things to Note When Pushing Projects to Git

Now that we've configured Truffle to use multiple networks, we can use those networks to modify our migration files. TestRPC automatically unlocks our accounts for us, so we don't have to do so explicitly. For security reasons, geth does not, so we will have to modify our migration file to explicitly do so.

Modify the `module.exports` callback in your migration file to look like Listing 3-6.

Listing 3-6. Unlocking Accounts in Migration Files

```
module.exports = function(deployer, network) {

    // unlock account for geth
    if (network == "rinkeby" || network == "mainnet") {
        var password = fs.readFileSync("password", "utf8")
                        .split('\n')[0];
        web3.personal.unlockAccount(web3.eth.accounts[0], password)
    }

    deployer.deploy(HelloWorld);
};
```

You'll notice that we load the password from an external file instead of importing it directly. This is important. *Do not input the password directly into the migration file.*

Caution The following are the most important few paragraphs in this book. Failure to follow these instructions exactly will most likely lead to your account being drained of all its ether. You have been warned.

When you commit and push your code to GitHub, all your code becomes publicly accessible. There are bots running around the Internet scraping public GitHub repositories, waiting on a naive soul to hard-code their API keys or passwords into their code. Remember when we said the only thing standing between the world and your private key when you run geth in RPC mode is your password? Well, putting that password on the Internet will pretty much guarantee that you will be hacked, and you would deserve it.

The proper way to protect not just this password, but any password or API key used in a script, is to place it in a gitignore file. `.gitignore` is the file git uses to determine which files to never commit to its repository. In your project root, create a `.gitignore` file and include Listing 3-7 as its contents.

Listing 3-7. Avoiding Cryptopoverty with a .gitignore File

```
build
password
```

We can now safely create the password file. In the project root, create a file called `password` and enter your password into it. The migration file will read in the password file to get the password. In the migration, to read the password file, we use the code `fs.readFileSync("password", "utf8").split('\n')[0];` to read the password instead of simply reading in the file. The reason for this is that most text editors will add in a newline character at the end of a file by default, and Node.js doesn't truncate this character. So this code splits the file into lines and then grabs the first line to avoid reading in extraneous characters.

> **Caution**   Beware the tale of Chad! Chad was a former student of mine who forgot to gitignore a file with his AWS keys. Hackers got ahold of his keys and used them to rack up $200,000 worth of charges on his AWS account in two months, likely to run Distributed Denial of Service, or DDoS, attacks for extortion. Don't be Chad. Gitignore your password file.

Summary	Amount
AWS Service Charges	$97,845.09
▶ Usage Charges and Recurring Fees View Invoices	$97,845.09
Other Details	
Total	$97,845.09

Summary	Amount
AWS Service Charges	$97,845.09
▶ Usage Charges and Recurring Fees View Invoices	$97,845.09
Other Details	
Total	$97,845.09

Summary	Amount
AWS Service Charges	$100,858.33
Other Details	
Total	$100,858.33

Figure 3-7.   *Chad waking up to a lifetime of debt*

Open the Rinkeby geth console in a separate terminal tab now and close any other running Ethereum clients. To allow local programs such as Truffle to execute transactions, we have to run geth in RPC mode.

From now on, all migrations to the testnet and mainnet have to run from the project root so the password file is available in the current directory. Attempt to deploy your contracts with Truffle, as shown in Listing 3-8.

Listing 3-8. Deploying Hello World to Rinkeby

```
# Tab 1
geth --rinkeby --rpc --rpcapi personal,web3,eth,net

# Tab 2
# Run from PROJECT_ROOT
truffle migrate -f 2 --network rinkeby
```

We use the same `migrate` command as before to deploy the contract, but this time it is preceded by the `truffle` command. This is because `migrate` is a subcommand of the `truffle` program. To use Truffle subcommands as standalone commands, they must be passed as the first argument to the `truffle` program. Any Truffle subcommand can also be called directly in the dev console. When called in the dev console, the `truffle` prefix is not required.

The `--network` flag is used to indicate that we wish to use the configurations for the Rinkeby network. If the deployment feels like it's taking a while, that's normal. The contract should take about 30 seconds to deploy. Once you've completed the deployment, complete Exercise 3-1 to practice interacting with the contract and Exercise 3-2 if you want to deploy the contract to the mainnet.

EXERCISE 3-1. GREETINGS FROM THE TESTNET

Use the Truffle console to access your deployed contract and run the greet function. Refer to the code in the "Private Chain" section if you can't remember the necessary commands.

EXERCISE 3-2. DEPLOYING TO THE MAINNET

Deploying to the mainnet is a similar process to deploying on the testnet. The `truffle.js` and migration files are already configured for a mainnet deployment. Try to deploy the Hello World contract to the mainnet by using Truffle.

Summary

In this chapter, we began working with one of the Ethereum testnets, creating addresses and initiating transactions from the command line. Then we manually deployed a smart contract to the testnet, and learned how to use the Truffle library to speed up the deployment process.

Finally, we went over basic precautions for using git for version control when building projects with Truffle. In the next chapter, we'll step back to discuss smart contracts in the abstract before diving into more hands-on examples.

CHAPTER 4

Smart Contracts in the Abstract

This chapter covers the theory behind smart contract programming, with a special focus on Truffle, Solidity, and the Ethereum protocol. The chapter is laid out in a fashion that allows it to be used as a reference while we're coding the games in the later chapters of the book. This chapter is intended for readers who have prior exposure to programming. Extensive experience is not required to understand the chapter, but new programmers should first go through a couple of Codecademy modules in JavaScript before reading this chapter (see `www.codecademy.com/learn/introduction-to-javascript`).

If you are the sort of person who prefers getting their hands dirty first and learning the theory as needed along the way, feel free to skip this chapter and lean on it as a reference going forward. For those who like to get a grasp on the theory behind a subject before jumping into practical applications, let's get started!

Truffle Theory

Truffle (`http://truffleframework.com/`) and Embark (`https://github.com/iurimatias/embark-framework`) are the two most popular development frameworks for Ethereum. We will be using Truffle in this book, but you are free to use Embark. Solidity code works equally well on both.

© Kedar Iyer and Chris Dannen 2018
K. Iyer and C. Dannen, *Building Games with Ethereum Smart Contracts*,
https://doi.org/10.1007/978-1-4842-3492-1_4

Truffle offers a powerful feature set for easily developing, testing, and deploying Solidity smart contracts. We used some many of the basic Truffle commands in the "Deploying with Truffle" section in Chapter 3. This section goes into more detail on those Truffle commands and highlights some new features that we have not used.

Configuration

Truffle can be configured to use any number of networks that run the Ethereum protocol. The configuration file is located at `truffle.js`.

We created three network configurations in the "Deploying with Truffle" section in Chapter 3. These network configurations will be reused for the remainder of the contracts in this book. The configuration we created there is reproduced in Listing 4-1.

Listing 4-1. Truffle Configuration File

```
module.exports = {
    networks: {
        development: {
            host: "localhost",
            port: 8545,
            network_id: "*" // Match any network id
        },
        rinkeby: {
            host: "localhost",
            port: 8545,
            network_id: 4
        },
        mainnet: {
            host: "localhost",
            port: 8545,
```

```
        network_id: 1
    }
  }
};
```

The three configurations are for the following networks: private chain (TestRPC), testnet (Rinkeby), and mainnet. Each network has the following options available, some of which we have not set:

- host: This is localhost for our local RPC node. An external IP or domain for a hosted node.

- port: The HTTP RPC port for the running node. TestRPC and geth use 8545 by default. If geth uses a custom port with the --rpcport flag, this configuration has to be updated to match.

- network_id: The network ID of the network—1 for mainnet, 4 for Rinkeby, and * to match any network.

- gas (optional): The default gas value to specify for transactions. Individual transactions can override this value. Default: 90000.

- gasPrice (optional): The default gas price for transactions in wei. Defaults to the mean network gas price. A good value if you wish to set this is 20 Gwei ($1 Gwei = 10^9$ wei). You can go as low as 1 Gwei and still have transactions clear within 10 minutes.

- provider (optional): An advanced configuration used to pass in a web3 provider. You will likely never use this.

In addition to networks, the configuration file can be used to set testing parameters. We will not be running tests in this book, but feel free to do so on your own. Truffle uses the Mocha test framework. To add test configurations, use the top-level key mocha. The full list of Mocha options can be found in the Mocha documentation (`https://github.com/mochajs/mocha/wiki`). Listing 4-2 is an example configuration for Mocha.

Listing 4-2. Test Configuration

```
module.exports = {
    networks: {...},
    mocha: {
        useColors: true
    }
};
```

By default, Truffle will not use the `solc` optimizer when compiling Solidity contracts. The optimizer reduces the size of contracts significantly to help you save on gas costs. Listing 4-3 demonstrates how to enable the optimizer.

Listing 4-3. Solc Optimizer Configuration

```
module.exports = {
    networks: {...},
    solc: {
        optimizer: {
            enabled: true,
            runs: 200
        }
    }
};
```

Migrations

Migrations are a Truffle construct for managing Ethereum deployments. Think of a migration as version control for deployments. Web developers who have used a web framework such as Rails will be familiar with the concept. Every migration has a number associated with it, and migrations are run in order of their number. After a migration has been run, it will not be run again unless explicitly forced. Migrations make it easy to replicate your deployments across multiple networks. You can test your deployments on a private chain and then rerun the same migrations on the mainnet.

A single migration is a JavaScript file containing deployment code. We wrote a simple Hello World migration in Listing 3-4. Take a moment to review that section if the details are fuzzy. Listing 4-4 is the standard migration template we will be using for our projects.

Listing 4-4. Standard Migration File

```
var fs = require('fs');
var Contract = artifacts.require("Contract");

module.exports = function(deployer, network) {

    // unlock account for geth
    if (network == "rinkeby" || network == "mainnet") {
        var password = fs.readFileSync("password", "utf8")
                        .split('\n')[0];
        web3.personal
            .unlockAccount(web3.eth.accounts[0], password)
    }

    deployer.deploy(Contract);
};
```

Replace Contract with the name of the contract you want to deploy and you'll have a migration file for that particular contract. If you want to deploy multiple contracts in a migration, require multiple contracts through the artifacts helper and run deployer.deploy once for each contract.

Migration files must export a callback that takes the deployer and network as its two arguments. All deployments must occur inside this callback. Internally, Truffle is importing all the migrations as a batch, and then executing their callbacks in order with the deployer and network arguments.

The deployer.deploy function can be used to pass in a series of constructor arguments. Listing 4-5 is a Token constructor that can be instantiated with a name and supply.

Listing 4-5. Example Token Contract Constructor

```
function Token(string _name, uint _totalSupply) public {
    name = _name;
    totalSupply = _totalSupply;
}
```

This Token contract requires two arguments to be instantiated. To deploy the contract in a migration, we would pass the required arguments to the deployer.deploy function:

```
deployer.deploy(Token, 'UnicornToken', 1e15)
```

We will see many more examples of this in the project chapters in the latter half of the book.

To run a migration, the command is truffle migrate. This runs the standard migration sequence, in which only new migrations are executed.

Our repository, however, will not use a typical linear development model. Each of our games will be a standalone contract or set of contracts that do not depend on the other games. To accommodate this structure, we will be abusing the Truffle migration flags to deploy games individually. A typical migration for us will look like this:

```
truffle migrate -f 2 --to 2
```

This line would run just migration #2. The -f flag forces the migrations to start at a specified number, and the --to flag specifies the last migration to be run.

Development Environment

Truffle has a built-in development environment console for quick debugging and testing. The command to run the console is as follows:

```
truffle develop
```

The dev environment runs a TestRPC private chain in the background. On initialization, it will create 10 keypairs and make them available to the user (Figure 4-1).

```
kedar@kedar-Latitude-E6430:~/code/ethereum-games$ truffle develop
Truffle Develop started at http://localhost:9545/

Accounts:
(0) 0x627306090abab3a6e1400e9345bc60c78a8bef57
(1) 0xf17f52151ebef6c7334fad080c5704d77216b732
(2) 0xc5fdf4076b8f3a5357c5e395ab970b5b54098fef
(3) 0x821aea9a577a9b44299b9c15c88cf3087f3b5544
(4) 0x0d1d4e623d10f9fba5db95830f7d3839406c6af2
(5) 0x2932b7a2355d6fecc4b5c0b6bd44cc31df247a2e
(6) 0x2191ef87e392377ec08e7c08eb105ef5448eced5
(7) 0x0f4f2ac550a1b4e2280d04c21cea7ebd822934b5
(8) 0x6330a553fc93768f612722bb8c2ec78ac90b3bbc
(9) 0x5aeda56215b167893e80b4fe645ba6d5bab767de

Mnemonic: candy maple cake sugar pudding cream honey rich smooth crumble sweet treat

truffle(develop)> █
```

Figure 4-1. *Truffle development console*

The console comes preloaded with a web3 connection from web3.js. Listing 4-6 demonstrates how to access accounts and block information by using web3.

Listing 4-6. web3 in the Console

```
web3.eth.accounts // view accounts
web3.eth.accounts[0] // get first account address

// view transaction receipt
web3.eth.getTransactionReceipt("0xfd8779e35e3b645ab3b3e6d7c2191
0f43841d940db7882ec09d9d3627de9501a")
```

All the standard Truffle commands are available in the console. The
truffle prefix is not required to run commands in the console. The
commands in Listing 4-7 are among the valid commands in the console.

Listing 4-7. Truffle Commands in the Console

```
compile
migrate
migrate -f 3 --to 3
```

In addition, we can access our deployed contracts. Let's say we want to
access the most recently deployed version of a Token contract. Listing 4-8
demonstrates how to do so.

Listing 4-8. Accessing Deployed Contracts in the Console

```
token = Token.at(Token.address) // contract instance
token.name // view name

// run transfer function
token.transfer(...)
```

Scripting

Running long or repetitive contract interactions in the console can be a
tedious affair. To make this easier, Truffle allows you to load scripts into the
dev console.

The command to execute a script in the Truffle environment is exec *script*, where *script* is a JavaScript file. The script can also be executed from the standard command-line prompt with truffle exec, but doing so requires running an Ethereum client in a separate tab. Because we will not be using any scripts in the book, we do not cover the details of how to do this.

Just as with migrations, any interactions with the blockchain in the script must go inside an exported callback function. If we wanted to execute the HelloWorld greet function in the Hello World contract from Chapter 3, we could do so with the code in Listing 4-9.

Listing 4-9. Hello World Truffle Script

```
HelloWorld = artifacts.require('HelloWorld');

module.exports = function () {
    instance = HelloWorld.at(HelloWorld.address);
    instance.greet().then(console.log);
}
```

Within the script, we can import contracts with artifacts.require and access deployed contracts as we do in the console.

Truffle scripting tends to be buggy and unintuitive, so we won't use any scripts in this book. If you're executing large amounts of automated code, the purpose is generally to run a test interaction, and doing so with Truffle tests is simpler and more powerful.

Most blockchain interactions will return a promise, so managing the flow of the promises becomes important in larger scripts and tests. Promises were touched on briefly in Chapter 3. If you've never worked with them before, check out the Google tutorial on JavaScript promises at https://developers.google.com/web/ilt/pwa/working-with-promises.

Tests

Although not a regular occurrence, this book occasionally provides automated test code for contracts. Test files can be found in the `test/` folder. Truffle supports tests written in both JavaScript and Solidity. The JavaScript tests use the web3.js library to interact with the blockchain, whereas the Solidity tests execute directly on the blockchain.

JavaScript testing uses the Mocha testing framework with Chai. This is one of the more popular test frameworks for JavaScript and comes with a clean, easy-to-use command-line interface. If you want to learn more, you can read the Mocha docs at `https://mochajs.org/`.

Solidity testing uses a built-in testing framework provided by Truffle. Solidity tests have access to a series of deployed contracts that can be used for testing. Both the JavaScript and Solidity run in a "clean-room" environment, meaning that every test runs on a fresh, sandboxed set of deployed contracts. Tests are free to make whatever modifications they want without affecting public or local deployments.

To run all test files at once, use the following command:

```
truffle test
```

Most of the time, we will be executing an individual test file focusing on a specific contract. To run an individual test file, here is the command:

```
truffle test path_to_file
```

As an example, to run the `test/reentrancy.js` test from the project root, use this command:

```
truffle test test/reentrancy.js
```

Ethereum Virtual Machine

In Chapter 1, you learned that the EVM is a platform on which all smart contract logic executes. The EVM itself is language agnostic; it executes bytecode generated by a compiler. As previously mentioned, we will be writing all our contracts in Solidity. EVM Assembly can be used inline with Solidity, but we will not be touching that beast in this book.

Standard CPUs have either 32-bit or 64-bit words. A *word* in computing is the size of the processor's register and size of a memory address. Virtual machines such as the JVM and EVM have word sizes as well. The EVM has a 256-bit (32-byte) word size. This is because memory addresses in the EVM state tree are Keccak256 hashes, which are 32 bytes long. The EVM state tree stores only nonzero values, so any variable in Solidity pointing to a nonexistent memory address is equal to the zero value for the data type. Table 4-1 in the "Zero Values" section contains the zero values for each data type.

Gas Fees

Every opcode in the EVM specification has an associated gas fee. An *opcode* is a single instruction on the EVM. For instance, the ADD opcode adds two numbers and costs three units of gas, whereas the SSTORE opcode stores one word of data into the state tree and costs 5,000 gas for a zero value and 20,000 gas for a nonzero value. Storing data on-chain is expensive.[1]

Refunds are given for operations that remove data from the state tree. The SSTORE opcode refunds 15,000 gas for removing a word of data from the state tree. Refunds are capped at half the gas costs of a transaction.

---

[1]https://ethereum.github.io/yellowpaper/paper.pdf

Solidity compiles into bytecode, which is actually just a series of opcode instructions for the EVM. The sum of the gas fees for the compiled bytecode instructions is the gas fee for the transaction.

Solidity Theory

Let's get an overview of Solidity by walking through the basics of control flow, functions, data storage, contracts, logging, and error handling.

Control Flow

The basic if, else, else if, for, and while control structures are available in Solidity with the exact same syntax as in C. Listing 4-10 gives an example using conditionals to pay out an over/under bet.

Listing 4-10. Control Flow with Conditionals

```
if (totalPoints > bet.line)
    balances[bet.over] += bet.amount * 2;
else if (totalPoints < bet.line)
    balances[bet.under] += bet.amount * 2;
else { // refunds for ties
    balances[bet.under] += bet.amount;
    balances[bet.over] += bet.amount;
}
```

Note that single-statement bodies can omit the brackets as in the if and else if portions, whereas the else body requires brackets because it has two statements. This is the same as in most C-inspired languages.

The for and while loops are used for repeating actions (Listing 4-11). The continue statement can be used to move to the next iteration in a loop, and the break statement can be used to break out of a loop. This implementation of loops is most similar to C.

Listing 4-11. Loops

```
// For loops
uint[] memory game_ids = new uint[](games.length);
for (uint i=0; i < games.length; i++) {
    game_ids[i] = (games[i].id);
}

for (uint i = 0; i < games.length; i++) {
    if (games[i].id == game_id) {
        Game game = games[i];
        break;
    }
}

// While loops
// Adding a bid to an exchange order book
uint insertIndex = stack.length;
while (insertIndex > 0 &&
        bid.limit <= stack[insertIndex-1].limit) {
    insertIndex--;
}
```

Function Calls in Solidity

Listing 4-12 is a basic addition function, as written in Solidity.

Listing 4-12. Basic Solidity Function

```
function add(uint a, uint b) public pure returns (uint) {
    return a + b;
}
```

Functions are declared with the keyword `function`, a name, a list of arguments, an optional list of modifiers, and an optional return type, in that order. Of these, all are standard in other languages except the modifiers. Modifiers are explained in more detail later in the chapter.

A function can return multiple values as well, as in Listing 4-13.

Listing 4-13. Returning Multiple Values

```
function getScore (Game game) public view returns
(uint home, uint away) {
    return (game.homeScore, game.awayScore);
}
```

Return types can be followed by an optional descriptive name to make the function definition clearer, as in the preceding function.

Function Visibility Modifiers

Visibility modifiers determine the contexts in which a function can be executed. There are four visibility modifiers in Solidity:

- `private`: Only the current contract can use the function.

- `internal`: Only the current contract and contracts inheriting from the current contract can execute the function.

- `external`: The function can be triggered only by a transaction or external contract.

- `public`: There are no restrictions on how the function can be called.

If no modifier is specified, the default visibility is public, but as a best practice, you should explicitly declare a visibility for each function. Doing so could have prevented the Parity multi-sig hack (see Chapter 5).

Only external and public functions are a part of the ABI. The ABI is discussed in more detail in the "Contract ABI" section.

State Permission Modifiers

Only some functions are permitted to modify the state tree. Functions declared with one of the following three modifiers cannot modify state or send ether:

- view: Can read information from the state tree but cannot modify state.

- pure: Cannot read or modify the state tree. The return value depends on only the function arguments.

- constant: An alias for view. Deprecated to prevent confusion with constant variables.

Although in theory you could declare all your functions without state permission modifiers to keep things simple, there's a huge advantage to using state permission modifiers. RPC calls to view or pure functions return immediately and don't send a transaction. This means you can get back the information you need without paying gas fees or waiting for the transaction to mine. Additionally, functions don't ordinarily return a value if called via transaction, so state permission modifiers are the only way to view return values in an Ethereum client.

Payable

The modifier payable is special, allowing functions to accept ether (Listing 4-14). Ordinary functions will throw an error if you attempt to send ether along with the function call. The amount of ether sent will be available in the msg.value field in units of wei.

Listing 4-14. Payable Functions

```
function buyLottoTicket() payable {
    require(msg.value == TICKET_PRICE);
    players.push(msg.sender);
}
```

Fallback Function

Every contract can have one unnamed function that acts as a default function to execute when no other functions can match the transaction call or when a transaction is sent to a contract without specifying a function. This function can be made payable so it accepts ether.

This function is generally used by contracts that are used for a single type of purchase, such as a crowdsale or lottery contract. It's convenient for users because they can simply send ether to an address and the function will execute. Listing 4-15 gives an example of a fallback function from the EOS crowdsale.

Listing 4-15. EOS Crowdsale Fallback Function

```
function () payable {
    buy();
}
```

Simple. Sending ether to the contract will execute the buy function. Users still have to make sure they are providing enough gas for the function to properly execute.

Contract ABI

The *contract ABI* (application binary interface) lists all the available functions in a contract. Only public and external functions are added to the ABI. Functions not in the ABI are inaccessible to outside contracts.

Ethereum uses JSON as the standard format for an ABI file. We created an ABI file when we compiled the Hello World contract in the "Manual Deployment" section of Chapter 3. Truffle handles the creation and loading of these files for us internally, so we don't have to worry about them for the most part.

To track a contract and execute contracts through an external wallet service, you need access to the ABI. You can find the ABIs for your contracts in the JSON files in `build/contracts/` under the key `abi`.

Working with Data

Data access and storage is the trickiest part of Solidity development. Because storage on the blockchain is expensive, Solidity has programming constructs designed to minimize storage fees. We will go through those constructs in this section after a quick overview of the data types built into the language.

Data Types

Solidity is a strongly typed language, so every variable has an associated data type. Let's walk through the list of data types available in Solidity. Most are standard, but some are unique to Solidity and Ethereum.

The `address` field is a 20-byte store specifically designed to hold Ethereum addresses (Listing 4-16). The address type has two members, `balance` and `transfer`, that can be used to check an address's balance and transfer its ether.

Listing 4-16. Using Address Types

```
address user = "0x801aa94F6B13DdF90447827eb905D7591b12eC79";
if (user.balance < 1 ether)
    user.transfer(1 ether);
```

The boolean type `bool` has only two possible values: `true` or `false`.

There are many integer types in Solidity: `int` is a signed 32-byte integer, and `uint` is an unsigned 32-byte integer. Also available are `int8` through `int256` by multiples of eight, and `uint8` through `uint256` by multiples of eight. So `int32` and `uint224` are valid, but `int55` is not. Integers can be assigned with both numbers and hex. All the assignments in Listing 4-17 are valid.

Listing 4-17. Integer Assignments

```
uint a = 32;
int b = 0x35bb;
uint8 c = uint8(a);
```

Solidity does not currently support floating- or fixed-point numbers, though that should change pretty soon. See Listing 4-29 for how to simulate decimal arithmetic with integers.

Solidity also supports multiple byte types: `bytes1` through `bytes32` are fixed-size byte arrays holding the specified number of bytes. `byte` is an alias for `bytes1`. `bytes` is a dynamically sized byte array. It must be initialized with an initial length. Arrays are covered in more detail in the next section.

All byte types have a property `.length` that gives the length of the byte array. For fixed-size byte arrays, the value is read-only. For the dynamically sized `bytes` type, the length property can be reassigned to lengthen or shorten the array. Listing 4-18 gives a couple of examples using byte types.

Listing 4-18. Byte Types

```
byte a = byte(1);

uint b = 0x1573593ab3;
bytes32 c = bytes32(b);
c.length; // 32

bytes d = new bytes(32);
d.length = 64; // d is now a 64 byte array
```

In this listing, `string` is an alias for `bytes` but it is interpreted by Solidity as a Unicode string. Solidity's string support is minimal (Listing 4-19). Basic functions such as string concatenation are not built into the language, and any string manipulation requires a conversion to `bytes`.

Listing 4-19. Solidity's (Lack of) String Support

```
string a = "hello";
string b = "world";
string c = a + b; // Error: string concatenation not supported
```

The type `enum` is an enumerable type for which only user-defined values are permitted. `enum` is explicitly convertible to integer types. The integer value of each enum is its zero-indexed order in the enum declaration (Listing 4-20).

Listing 4-20. Enumerables

```
enum State { Active, Refunding, Closed }
State state = State.Refunding;
uint(state); // 1
uint(State.Active) // 0
```

The type `mapping` is Solidity's version of a hashmap. It's a key/value store in which both the key and the value must adhere to the specified data type. The value can be any data type, whereas the key type is restricted to `address`, `bool`, the integer types, fixed-size arrays, and the fixed-size byte types. The most common use case for a mapping is to store internal balances of token or ether.

```
mapping(address => uint) public balances;
balances[msg.sender] += 10;
```

Every key in a mapping is hashed to a unique address in the state tree, so in theory a `mapping` can be as large as the entire state tree (2^{256} keys), and every key is initialized to the zero value of the data type. Unfortunately, this also means there is no way to obtain the set keys for a mapping or differentiate between unset values and zero values. You will have to maintain a separate array if you wish to track set keys.

Arrays

A sequence of any data type, including structs, can be created with arrays. Solidity supports both fixed-size and dynamic arrays. All arrays have a .length property. For fixed-size arrays, .length is read-only. Dynamic arrays can be resized by setting the .length property. Items can also be appended to a dynamic array with .push to automatically lengthen the array by 1. Common array examples are given in Listing 4-21.

Listing 4-21. Arrays

```
uint[3] ids; // empty fixed size array
uint[] x; // empty dynamic array
x.push(2);
x.length; // 1
x.length += 1; // adds a zero value element
```

Structs

When the preceding types do not suffice, or a more complex data type is required, Solidity supports struct, similar to a C struct (Listing 4-22).

Listing 4-22. Structs

```
struct Bet {
    uint amount; /* in wei */
    int32 line;
    BetStatus status; /* enum */
}
Bet memory bet = Bet(1 ether, -1, BetStatus.Open);
bet.line; // -1
```

The struct type defines a complex data type that has other data types as members. Any data type can appear in a struct, and nesting structs is permitted. Declaring a struct creates a constructor that can be used to instantiate instances of that struct. Struct members are accessed with the . notation (bet.line, bet.amount, etc.).

Zero Values

The *zero value* is the default value for an uninitialized variable. Every data type has an associated zero value. Table 4-1 lists the zero values for each data type.

Table 4-1. *Zero Values for Solidity Data Types*

Data Type(s)	Zero Value
Integer types	0
bool	false
address	0x0
Byte types	0
Array	[ ] (length = 0)
mapping	No keys

For a struct, each individual member will be initialized to its own zero value.

Variables set or initialized to the zero value in Solidity are not included in the state tree. The delete keyword in Solidity resets a variable to its zero value and deletes the variable from the state tree.

Variable Visibility Modifiers

There are two types of variables, state and local. *State variables* are generally declared in the global contract scope. *Local variables* are declared within a function and destroyed when the function is complete. State variables can be declared public, private, or internal, but they cannot be declared external. See the previous "Visibility Modifiers" section for a description of those terms.

Solidity automatically generates a getter ABI function for all public state variables. For arrays and mappings, the getter takes one argument, corresponding to the index and the key, respectively. The getter functions are view functions, so do not require a transaction to access. Listing 4-23 is a Bear contract we will use to demonstrate getters.

Listing 4-23. Variable Types and Getters

```
contract Bear {
    // state variables
    string public name = "gummy";
    uint internal id = 1;

    function touchMe (uint times) public pure returns (bool)
    {
        bool touched = false; // local variable
        if (times > 0) touched = true;
        return touched;
    }
}
```

In this case, Solidity would generate a getter function for name, but not id or touched.

Storage vs. Memory

Solidity stores locations in two places: in the state tree and in memory. Storage in the state tree persists on the blockchain, whereas the memory is cleared after every transaction. Storage on the state tree is expensive and should be used only when necessary. Memory is cheap and should be used whenever possible. Solidity refers to these two locations as storage for the state tree and memory for memory. We do the same going forward.

Local variables that aren't arrays or structs and all state variables are automatically forced into storage. For local arrays and structs, we can choose where to store the variable. Arrays and structs in function arguments default to memory, whereas local arrays and structs default to storage. Both of these can be overridden when necessary by explicitly declaring the variable with the keywords storage or memory. Examples of each of these situations are available in Listing 4-24.

Listing 4-24. Basic Data Locations

```
contract Airbud {
    // state variables forced to storage
    address[] users;
    mapping(address => uint) public balances;

    function yelp () public payable {
        // local variable defaults to storage
            address user = msg.sender;

        // local variable declared to memory
        uint8[3] memory ids = [1,2,3];
    }
}
```

Because data location declarations are not found in other languages, we make it a point to clearly explain the uses of the memory and storage keywords in our code as we go along.

Contract Structure

The modular unit of Solidity code is the contract. A *contract* works similarly to a class in classical programming. Contracts can inherit from one another, and modifiers can be used to mix in functionality.

Inheritance

The closest parallel to Solidity's inheritance system is Python. Solidity supports multiple inheritance by using the is keyword. If a function or variable is not available in a child contract, Solidity will check the parent contract for the function before throwing an error. A basic inheritance structure is shown in Listing 4-25.

Listing 4-25. Contract Inheritance

```
contract owned {
    function owned() { owner = msg.sender; }
    address owner;
}

contract mortal is owned {
    function kill() {
        if (msg.sender == owner) selfdestruct(owner);
    }
}
```

Here, mortal inherits from owned. When the kill function attempts to access the owner variable, Solidity uses the instance declared in the owned contract because mortal does not have an owner variable in either the local or global scope.

This is as complex as we get with inheritance in this book. If you would like to know more about inheritance in Solidity, you can read the docs (http://solidity.readthedocs.io/en/develop/contracts.html#inheritance) and check out the OpenZeppelin StandardToken contract, which uses multiple inheritance (https://github.com/OpenZeppelin/zeppelin-solidity/blob/master/contracts/token).

Modifiers

We talked earlier about function modifiers in Solidity and how they can be used to set visibility and state permissions. Solidity allows the creation of custom modifiers as well with the keyword `modifier`. Let's rewrite our inheritance code so that it uses a modifier to restrict access to the `kill` function to the owner of the contract (Listing 4-26).

Listing 4-26. Function Modifiers

```
contract owned {
    function owned() { owner = msg.sender; }
    address owner;

    modifier onlyOwner {
        require(msg.sender == owner);
        _;
    }
}

contract mortal is owned {
    function kill() onlyOwner {
        selfdestruct(owner);
    }
}
```

Contracts inherit all custom modifiers from parent contracts. The modifier onlyOwner is used to make sure the sender of the transaction is the owner. Modifiers wrap the function that calls them and can use _; to yield execution to the original function—in this case, kill. Listings 4-25 and 4-26 represent the exact same functionality in two forms.

Logging and Events

Ethereum has two independent top-level data structures. The first is the one we always talk about: the state tree. The second, a log database, is rarely mentioned. Solidity contracts can write to both data structures, but they can read only from the state tree.

Logs are used either as a trigger for UI actions or as a form of cheap storage. Solidity has an easy-to-use interface for logging called *Events* with a syntax similar to structs. Listing 4-27 demonstrates a Withdrawal event.

Listing 4-27. Logging with Events

```
event Withdrawal(
    address indexed user,
    uint amount,
    uint timestamp
);

function withdraw (uint amount) public {
    Withdrawal(msg.sender, amount, now);
}
```

Events are declared with the keyword event followed by a name for the event. By convention, event names are capitalized. Every field in an event must have a data type and name. There is no limit to the number of fields you can have in an event. Up to three fields in an event can be marked and indexed with the keyword indexed. Front-end clients can run queries directly on indexed columns. With the event generated by Listing 4-27, we would be able to query the blockchain for all withdrawals by a given user.

Solidity exposes a low-level log interface as well for direct logging with the functions log0, log1...log4, but you should be using events.

Operators and Built-in Functions

Listing 4-28 lists the available arithmetic operators in Solidity. The operators are similar to those in Python.

Listing 4-28. Arithmetic Operators

```
uint a = 3;

2 + 3; // addition
a += 3; // shorthand for a = a + 3
a++; // shorthand for a += 1

3 - 2; // subtraction
a -= 1; // shorthand for a = a -1

a--; // shorthand for a -= 1
3 * 2; // multiplication
a *= 3; // shorthand for a = a * 3

4 / 2; // integer division
3 / 2; // = 1, no floating point arithmetic
a /= 2; // shorthand for a = a / 2;
10 % 2; // modulus

2**3; // power operator, this is 2³
2e7; // scientific notation, this is 2 * 10⁷
```

It's important to note that because there are no floating-point numbers in Solidity, all division is integer division, and decimals are truncated. To get decimal precision, you use the workaround similar to Listing 4-29.

Listing 4-29. Decimal Precision with Integer Division

```
uint a = 10;
uint b = 3;

// multiply by 10**n to add n zeros
// if you add n zeros, the last n digits will
// be the decimal digits
uint c = (a * 10**6) / b; // 3333333
```

We added six zeros, so the last six digits are decimal digits, and the true answer is 3.333333. We will be using this workaround extensively in our games.

Numbers must be the same type to be operated on together. Mismatched types throw an error (Listing 4-30).

Listing 4-30. Type Matching with Operators

```
uint a = 10;
uint b = 3;
int c = 5;
a * b; // 30
b * c; // Error: type mismatch
```

Solidity comes with built-in time units to make working with time easy. The units seconds, minutes, hours, days, weeks, and years are all automatically converted into a uint equivalent of seconds. Listing 4-31 lists some time equalities.

Listing 4-31. Time Comparisons

```
1 == 1 seconds;
60 seconds == 1 minutes;
3600 seconds ==  1 hour;
1 year == 365 days;
```

The now keyword can be used to get the UNIX timestamp (seconds after the UNIX epoch of 1970-01-01 00:00:00). This makes it easy to create delayed actions, as in Listing 4-32.

Listing 4-32. Time-Delayed Actions

```
contract TimedPayout {
    uint start;

    function TimedPayout () payable {
        start = now;
    }

    function claim () {
        if (now > start + 10 days)
            msg.sender.transfer(address(this).balance)
    }
}
```

Any money sent to the contract when it is deployed can be claimed in 10 days by the first person to run the claim transaction.

Solidity has currency units, which we've used multiple times already without explanation. The keywords wei (10^{-18} ether), finney (10^{-3} ether), szabo (10^{-6} ether), and ether are supported, but finney and szabo are rarely used. Most code, including ours, sticks with ether and wei. The currency units are all converted into uint of wei, the smallest denomination of ether. msg.value, a built-in function, stores the amount of wei sent to a payable function. Some examples of currency math are provided in Listing 4-33.

Listing 4-33. Currency Math

```
1 == 1 wei;
1 ether ==  10**18 wei;
2 ether == 2e18 wei;
2 finney == .002 ether;
if (msg.value == 1 ether) buyLottoTicket();
msg.value; // 1000000000000000000 a.k.a. 1 ether
```

The following are some of the built-in variables available in
the global namespace. For a full list, see the Solidity docs (http://
solidity.readthedocs.io/en/develop/units-and-global-variables.
html#special-variables-and-functions).

- block.number (uint): The current block number/
  height.

- now (uint): Current UNIX timestamp.

- tx.origin (address): The address of the initiator of a
  transaction.

- msg.sender (address): The address of the sender of
  a function call. Different from tx.origin. When one
  contract calls another contract, tx.origin is the address
  of the user who sent the transaction, and msg.sender is
  the address of the first contract. tx.origin is always a
  wallet address. msg.sender can be a contract address.

- msg.value: Number of wei sent to a payable function.
  Always 0 for nonpayable functions.

- this: The current contract type (its name).
  address(this) returns the address of the current
  contract.

- this.balance: Alias for address(this).balance. Ether
  balance of the current contract.

In addition to global variables, here are some of the useful global functions:

- `keccak256(...)`: Takes any number of arguments of any data type, converts them in order to a single-byte sequence, and then computes the Keccak256 hash of the byte sequence. This is the default hash function used by the EVM.

- `sha256(...)`: Computes the SHA-256 hash of the arguments.

- `ripemd160(...)`: Computes the RIPEMD-160 hash of the arguments.

- `selfdestruct(address recipient)`: Removes the current contract and all associated data from the state tree. Refunds any remaining ether, `this.balance`, to the recipient.

Error Handling

When a smart contract throws an error, all changes made to the state tree during the current transaction are rolled back. The code can decide whether to refund any unused gas. For errors that imply malicious intent, it is best to consume the unused gas, whereas common errors should refund gas.

The `revert` function throws a manual error and refunds all unused gas. `require(condition)` and `assert(condition)` throw an error and consume all unused gas if *condition* is false. As of this writing, `throw` is an old form of error handling that has been deprecated. You may see it in older code snippets.

The assert error is used to check for internal consistency. Properly functioning code should never throw an assert error. If it does, your code has a bug. When in doubt, use require to check input conditions. It's up to you; using one over the other will not create security flaws in your contract.

The different error-handling mechanisms are demonstrated in Listing 4-34.

Listing 4-34. Error Handling

```
contract BugSquash {
    enum State { Alive, Squashed }
    State state;
    address owner;

    function BugSquash () {
        state = State.Alive;
        owner = msg.sender;
    }

    function squash () {
        // this should never throw an error
        assert(owner != address(0));

        if (state == State.Alive)
            state = State.Squashed;
        else if (state == State.Squashed)
            revert(); // user error, refund gas
    }
```

```
function kill () {
    // any nonowner trying to kill the contract
    // likely has malicious intent
    require(msg.sender == owner);
    selfdestruct(owner);
    }
}
```

Ethereum Protocol

While we use the RPC server to communicate with our geth instance, nodes on the network communicate with each other via the Ethereum wire protocol. The RPC server exposes a good deal, but not all, of the wire protocol functionality to external clients. The exact specifications for the Ethereum protocol can be found on GitHub at https://github.com/ethereum/wiki/wiki/Ethereum-Wire-Protocol.

Ethereum is a peer-to-peer protocol. Ethereum clients maintain a list of peers with whom they share block and transaction information. Broadcasting a transaction or block involves sending the appropriate message to each of the peers on the peer list, each of whom then forward the information onto their peer list until all peers on the network have received the information. Consensus is enforced during this process by refusing to accept or propagate malformed blocks or transactions.

Note   Remote procedure call (RPC) is the concept of invoking a computing procedure, function, or program on a remote computer. HTTP, the protocol of the web browser, is a form of RPC, but there are many other forms. Ethereum uses JSON-RPC, a simple form of RPC that sends JSON terminated by an endline character to invoke remote commands.

Summary

In this chapter, we have gone over the fundamentals of using Truffle and the Solidity programming language to code, test, and deploy smart contracts to the Ethereum Virtual Machine. Here's a quick overview.

Control structures in Solidity are similar to those in JavaScript. The standard conditional and loop structures available in other languages are implemented in a similar fashion in Solidity.

Functions in Solidity can use modifiers to control the visibility of the function, restrict access to the state tree, and accept ether. Custom modifiers can be written to perform other modifications. Contracts can define a fallback function that acts as the default function for the contract.

Data can be stored in memory, in the state tree, or in the log database. Memory is the cheapest but doesn't persist. Logs are still cheap but are write-only and can't be read by smart contracts. The state tree is expensive but offers full read and write access. Variables can be designated as belonging to either memory or storage.

All the standard arithmetic operators are available in Solidity. In addition, time and currency arithmetic are supported with convenient units and conversions. Floating-point numbers are not supported, so workarounds must be used for decimal arithmetic.

Transactions in Ethereum are atomic, so throwing an error in your code will revert all state changes and log entries made by the transaction. Errors can be thrown in ways that either consume or refund unused gas.

When the contract code is ready, Truffle can be used to compile the contracts. Truffle migrations must be written and executed to deploy the contracts. The contracts can be deployed to a private chain, the testnet, or the mainnet. We have configured our project so that it is ready to do all three.

You now know enough about Solidity to construct your first Ethereum games. In the next chapter, we will cover contract security and how to write safe code that can't be hacked.

CHAPTER 5

Contract Security

Strong security is the foundation of blockchain technology. Without it, blockchains offer no advantage over traditional software. This chapter, covers security best practices for Solidity. Security of the Ethereum blockchain itself is covered in Chapter 6. Thousands of ether have been lost or hacked from smart contracts because of poorly written code. Following the best practices in this chapter will minimize the chances of that happening to your own contracts.

Note   This is the most complex chapter in the book. If you can work your way through the examples in this chapter, the remainder of the book gets easier from here.

All Contract Data Is Public!

All data on the blockchain is public. Any data stored in the Ethereum state tree can be read from a node's local copy.

In Chapter 4, we talked about private functions and variables. Private functions and variables cannot be accessed by other contracts or external clients, but that doesn't mean the contents are completely hidden. Block explorers will generally respect visibility rules and refuse to display private data, but don't be fooled into complacency because your private data doesn't show up on Etherscan.

© Kedar Iyer and Chris Dannen 2018
K. Iyer and C. Dannen, *Building Games with Ethereum Smart Contracts*,
https://doi.org/10.1007/978-1-4842-3492-1_5

Every contract has a designated storage space, a subtree within the main state tree. Review the contract in Listing 5-1 and then try Exercise 5-1.

Listing 5-1. Not-So-Private Variables

```
contract NotSoPrivateData {
    uint public money = 16;
    uint public constant lives = 100;
    string private password = "twiddledee";
}
```

EXERCISE 5-1. DEPLOYMENT

Deploy the contract in Listing 5-1 to the Rinkeby testnet. Note the contract address, as we will be using it soon.

To access the contract storage, we will use web3.eth.getStorage At(contractAddress, index). The contract address will be the address of the deployed contract in Exercise 5-1. If you skipped that exercise, we have a deployed version at 0x3400daf738b1b26451cea087bdcffa919d1c04d8 that you can use. The index comes from the order of the variables in the contract. Constant variables are hard-coded into the contract bytecode and don't get an index, so lives will not have an index. In our contract, money and password would have indices 0 and 1, respectively.

Open a Rinkeby geth console and enter the code in Listing 5-2. Each line of user-entered text is followed by the return value displayed by geth.

Listing 5-2. Accessing Contract Storage

```
> contractAddress = "0x3400daf738b1b26451cea087bdcffa919d1c04d8"
undefined
> web3.eth.getStorageAt(contractAddress, 0)
"0x0000000000000000000000000000000000000000000000000000000000000010"
> web3.eth.getStorageAt(contractAddress, 1)
"0x74776964646c65646565000000000000000000000000000000000000
000000014"
```

Remember that all values in the Ethereum state tree are 32-byte words. If you check the length of the returned hex values, you will see that they are 64 characters long, corresponding to 32 bytes of storage. The value of the first index is 0x10, which is 16 in decimal. This matches the value of our first public variable, money.

Solidity uses Unicode UTF-8 to encode strings. Short strings fewer than 31 bytes long are stored in a single word. The last byte indicates the length (L) of the string in nibbles, while the string itself is stored in the first L nibbles. A *nibble* is half a byte, or one hexadecimal character. Our last byte is 0x14, so the string is 20 nibbles, or 10 bytes long. The first 20 nibbles of the word are 0x74776964646c65646565, which decodes to the Unicode string "twiddledee".

This corresponds to the value of our password variable. But wait! Our password was supposed to be private! Now you know, nothing in Ethereum is truly private.

As expected, the constant variable lives was skipped. This does not mean it is safely hidden, though, as the value can be decoded from the contract bytecode. Go to the Etherscan code page for the deployed contract at https://rinkeby.etherscan.io/address/0x3400daf738b1 b26451cea087bdcffa919d1c04d8#code, select the Opcodes view for the Contract Creation code, and scroll to the bottom. As in Figure 5-1, you will see that the hex value for the constant variable, 0x64, is pushed into storage. Decoding EVM Assembly is outside the scope of this book, so we do not cover how to determine which statement corresponds to which variable except to note that a sufficiently motivated attacker could figure it out.

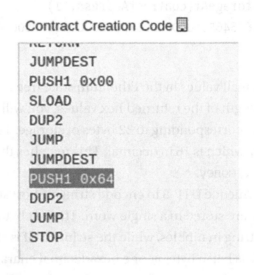

Figure 5-1. *Finding constants in bytecode*

Complex data types and long strings are not as easy to decode as short strings or simple data types such as uint. If you're interested in reading more, you can find the full spec for storing variables in storage at http://solidity.readthedocs.io/en/latest/miscellaneous.html#layout-of-state-variables-in-storage.

All complex data types are decodable directly from contract storage, except mapping. There is no way to determine the keys of a mapping directly from its layout in storage (see the above link for more details). However, because all transactions are public and deterministic, if you have access to the source code and every transaction that interacted with the contract, you can determine which keys have already been set. It may not be simple, but it is doable. Determining the keys of a mapping from within a smart contract without maintaining a separate list is still not possible, though, and this is a problem we will struggle with later.

Lost Ether

It is possible to send ether in a way that it is irrevocably lost. Both addresses and contracts can lose their ether.

Addresses

The simplest way to lose your ether is to lose all copies of your private key. Your private key is required to sign any transaction sending your ether, so if you lose all copies of the key, you can no longer access your ether.

The best way to avoid this is to back up your key. If possible, you should back up your seed phrase instead of your key. Most wallets use a seed phrase to generate a fresh key for every transaction. Generating a fresh key for every transaction makes it harder to trace the owner of an address by using link analysis. The seed phrase is in plain English, so it is a lot easier to identify any small copying errors you might make while backing up the key.

Most security experts will warn you against creating a digital backup of your seed. If possible, a paper backup is always the safest method because it can't be hacked or compromised. However, if you are the forgetful type or don't trust yourself to not lose the paper, a digital backup is better than no backup.

The safest way to perform a digital backup is to take two pictures, each with half your seed words, and save the files in separate folders in an encrypted external drive or your local hard drive. Saving a text version of your words makes it a lot easier for a virus to parse the file and determine that it contains a seed phrase or private key. Most viruses will not have access to sophisticated image-recognition technology. In case virus creators get smarter, splitting your seed words into two images will add one more layer of security.

Do not upload these images to any Internet service. Hacks happen to cloud providers every day, and if a hacker realizes what they have their hands on, you are utterly screwed.

Aside from losing keys, ether can be lost by sending it to an invalid or nonexistent address. Most software including geth uses a capitals-based checksum to prevent invalid addresses from being used. A *checksum* is a mechanism for making sure entered addresses are valid.

Checksummed addresses using mixed-cased letters were introduced in Ethereum in EIP 55.[1] To generate an address checksum, create a binary Keccack256 hash of the standard address. If a character in the standard address at index i is a letter (a–f), and the binary hash contains a 1 at index 4*i, capitalize that letter. More simply, what this is does is go through an address and pseudorandomly but reproducibly capitalize half the letters. Using this system, there is only a 1-in-5,000 chance that a mistyped address will be valid.

To benefit from checksums, make sure any address you are sending ether or tokens to contains both capital and lowercase letters. Addresses with just lowercase letters are not checksummed, so a single miscopy or typo can result in your ether being sent into the void.

Contracts

While using geth, the most common way of losing ether is by forgetting to include the to field in a transaction. This will send the ether to the null address and attempt a contract creation. With no data, an empty contract is created containing your ether, and your ether is lost forever. The most notorious example of this occurred when the price of ether was less than

---

[1]Github, "Ethereum Improvement Proposal 55", https://github.com/ethereum/EIPs/blob/master/EIPS/eip-55.md, April 4, 2018

$1 on the this transaction at `https://etherscan.io/tx/0x7614ee2f5dee de9748a8c19f092100369a7fc5c59bae8e1938b50c779eb7afa0`. That 1,000 ether is now worth hundreds of thousands of dollars as of this writing.

Another common error is sending contract creation data to the zero address instead of the null address. To avoid this, don't require your contracts to be funded on creation. Separate the two processes. If you accidentally do send data to the zero address, you will now lose only your gas fee. To view a list of people who have lost ether to the zero address, you can view the Etherscan page for the zero address (`https://etherscan.io/ address/0x0000000000000000000000000000000000000000`). Think of it as the Ethereum Darwin Awards.

Self-destructing contracts can sometimes lead to problems. If a user sends ether to a self-destructed contract, that ether is impossible to reclaim. To prevent this, contracts can be designed so that they can be suspended instead of self-destructed. Suspended contracts reject all attempts at interaction and permit only withdrawals. We will go over suspending contracts later in the chapter.

Storing Ether in Contracts

All ether sent to a contract is stored in the contract and can be dispersed only by a contract function that sends the ether to a new address or self-destructs the contract. Failing to code output methods will lead to the ether being stuck in the contract forever.

Ether can be sent only to `payable` contract functions. If ether is sent to a contract address without transaction data, the send is rejected unless the contract has a `payable` fallback function.

If a contract has no `payable` functions, this does not mean it is guaranteed to have a contract balance of zero. Ether can still be credited to the contract by invoking `selfdestruct(`*address*`)` in a second contract with the first contract's address. All ether stored in the second contract will be sent to the first contract, and this action cannot be rejected. If the first contract does not contain any output methods, the ether in the contract is lost.

The easiest way to avoid these problems is to minimize the amount of ether held in contracts. If a contract does not require funds on hand, withdraw them at regular intervals. If a contract stores user balances, try to safely send the user their funds before storing a balance. If a contract has served its purpose, self-destruct it if possible and get any extra funds out. What isn't there can't be stolen, so get ether out of a contract as soon as possible.

Sending Ether

Improper use of the ether transfer functions are the number one source of Solidity bugs and hacks. There are three ways to send ether in Solidity:

- *address*.transfer(*value*)
- *address*.send(*value*)
- *address*.call.value(*value*)()

If the transfer fails, *address*.transfer throws an error, and *address*.send returns false. If the receiver *address* is a contract address, all three of these functions will trigger the receiving contract's fallback function. Both *address*.transfer and *address*.send provide a fixed gas stipend of 2,300 gas, which is just enough to log an event and nothing more. If you want to provide more gas to a contract recipient, *address*.call.value will forward all unused gas to the participant.

Caution   Using *address*.call.value opens you up to re-entrancy attacks, which are discussed later in the chapter. This was a crucial part of the DAO hack, which lost millions of ether.

Unless you have a good reason to do otherwise, you should use
.transfer because it is the most secure. Listing 5-3 displays the simplest
form of payout, sending the whole balance of a contract to an address.

Listing 5-3. Transfer Contract Balance to a Single User

```
address receiver = address(15); // dummy address
function payout () {
    uint balance = address(this).balance;
    receiver.transfer(balance);
}
```

This is the simplest way of sending ether out of your contract. Grab
the whole balance and send it to a receiver's address. If there is only one
receiver and that receiver is a wallet address, this will suffice.

If the receiver is a contract address, the transfer function will try to
execute the fallback function. If the fallback function does not exist or
is not marked payable, the transfer will throw an error, and the payout
function cannot execute. Additionally, .transfer provides only 2,300 gas
to the fallback function, so if it consumes more gas than that, it will fail
with an OutOfGasError.

This is not a major problem if the function has no other purpose than
to make the payout. It is the responsibility of each contract creator to
create proper fallback functions if they wish to receive ether. However,
if a function has multiple transfers or performs other state updates as in
Listing 5-4, those transfers and updates will be rolled back along with the
failed transfer. Attackers can take advantage of this to lock up a contract
and prevent it from reaching a desired state.

Listing 5-4. Poorly Coded Transfers to Multiple Recipients

```
// DO NOT USE: BAD CODE
contract TrustFund {
    address[3] children;

    function TrustFund (address[3] _children) {
        children = _children;
    }

    function updateAddress(uint child, address newAddress)
    {
        require(msg.sender == children[child]);
        children[child] = newAddress;
    }

    function disperse () {
      uint balance = address(this).balance;
      children[0].transfer(balance / 2);
      children[1].transfer(balance / 4);
      children[2].transfer(balance / 4);
    }

    function () payable {}
}
```

Listing 5-4 sets up a TrustFund contract in which one child gets half the money, and the other two children get one-quarter each. It has an empty payable fallback function that can be used to fund the contract, and an updateAddress function so that children can update their addresses.

If I'm the second child and I'm upset that I'm not receiving my fair share, I can lock up the contract so that no one can access their funds by updating my address to an empty contract with no fallback function:

```
contract SaltyChild {}
```

Because this contract is empty and has no fallback function, it will reject any ether sent to its address. Now when the first child tries to access his funds by running the disperse function, he will find that the failed transfer to the second child rolls back all three transfers, and nobody can access their funds.

Listing 5-5 solves this particular case by modifying our disperse function to use .send instead of .transfer.

Listing 5-5. Safely Dispersing Ether to a Fixed Number of Addresses

```
function disperse () {
    uint balance = address(this).balance;
    children[0].send(balance / 2);
    children[1].send(balance / 4);
    children[2].send(balance / 4);
}
```

Now instead of throwing an error, .send will return false for the second child, and everybody else will be able to receive their ether.

This solution for a fixed number of addresses does not generalize to one in which the number of transfers is high and unknown. Listing 5-6 creates a contract representing such a situation.

Listing 5-6. Sending Ether to a Large Number of Addresses: UNSAFE

```
// DO NOT USE: BAD CODE
contract Welfare {
    address[] recipients;

    function register () {
        recipients.push(msg.sender);
    }

    function disperse () {
        uint balance = address(this).balance;
        uint amount = balance / recipients.length;
        for (uint i=0; i < recipients.length; i++) {
            recipients[i].send(amount);
        }
    }

    function () payable {}
}
```

Just as in our previous contract, this contract is fundable by sending ether to the address. This time, however, anybody is free to register for a payout, and the number of recipients is unknown. We have used the `.send` method to transfer money, so a single recipient can't hold up the whole queue.

But what if too many people sign up? Each send operation consumes 9,000 gas. If 1,000 people register, the `disperse` function will require 9 million gas. The block gas limit is currently about 7 million. The `disperse` function will throw an `OutOfGasError` when executed. An attacker can take advantage of this to spam the contract and register a bunch of dummy addresses. This will lock the ether in the contract.

To avoid these problems, best practice in Solidity is to use a withdraw function with internal balances. Let's see how that looks in the next section.

Withdraw Methods

A withdraw function performs only one transfer per transaction. Combined with internal balances, this ensures that errors thrown by transfers lock only the ether of the malicious/incompetent user. Listing 5-7 displays how a simple Roulette contract would implement internal balances.

Note   Listing 5-7 follows best practices and can be used safely in your contracts.

Listing 5-7. Internal Balances

```
// GOOD CODE!
contract Roulette {
    mapping(address => uint) balances;

    function betRed () payable {
        winner = (randomNumber() % 2 == 0);
        if (winner)
            balances[msg.sender] += msg.value * 2;
    }

    function randomNumber() returns (uint) {
        // we will implement this in a later section
        // for now, imagine it returns a number from
        // 0-36
    }
```

```
function withdraw () {
    uint amount = balances[msg.sender];
    balances[msg.sender] = 0;
    msg.sender.transfer(amount);
  }
}
```

The contract maintains an internal mapping of balances. There is no limit to the number of addresses this mapping can store. When a user wins a bet, instead of directly transferring them ether, the internal balance is updated. The user can then withdraw their ether in a separate transaction.

This specific contract can actually be written safely without the withdraw code. If the betRed function is written as in Listing 5-8, the withdraw code and internal balances become unnecessary.

Listing 5-8. An Alternate Safe Roulette Implementation

```
function betRed () payable {
    bool winner = (randomNumber() % 2 == 0);
    if (winner)
        msg.sender.transfer(msg.value * 2);
}
```

To be safe, it is best to use the withdraw method. Using a direct payout requires you to think carefully through the possible attack vectors every time. The withdraw method in Listing 5-7 is safe and will always work.

Let's go back to the Welfare contract now. How would we design it so it works as intended? We can't directly store internal balances for every user each time a funding occurs, for the same reason we can't make 1,000 transfers: gas costs. The SSTORE opcode to store or update one word of storage consumes 20,000 gas. Updating 1,000 balances would consume 20 million gas, far exceeding the block gas limit. Instead, we will track the total funding and individual amounts each user has withdrawn in Listing 5-9.

Listing 5-9. Sending Ether Safely to a Large Number of Recipients

```
contract Welfare {
    address[] recipients;
    uint totalFunding;
    mapping(address => uint) withdrawn;

    function register () {
        recipients.push(msg.sender);
    }

    function () payable {
        totalFunding += msg.value;
    }

    function withdraw () {
        uint withdrawnSoFar = withdrawn[msg.sender];
        uint allocation = totalFunding / recipients.length;
        require(allocation > withdrawnSoFar);

        uint amount = allocation - withdrawnSoFar;
        withdrawn[msg.sender] = allocation;
        msg.sender.transfer(amount);
    }
}
```

The allocation is calculated as an even distribution of the total funding to each user. The withdraw function requires the allocation to be greater than the amount withdrawn by the user. If it is, the allocation is sent to the user. In this design, each transfer occurs in an individual transaction, so there is no limit to the number of recipients the contract can handle. Furthermore, the balances are tracked by updating a withdrawn mapping during the withdrawal phase, so no more than one state update occurs per transaction as well.

Up to this point, we have used only .transfer and .send to send ether. When a contract address attempts a withdrawal, both these functions allocate the external fallback function only 2,300 gas. What if we wanted contracts with complex fallback functions to be able to withdraw ether? Listing 5-10 lists such a contract that splits balances between two users.

Listing 5-10. Complex Fallback Function

```
contract Marriage () {
    address wife = address(0); // dummy address
    address husband = address(1); // dummy address

    function withdraw () {
        uint amount = balances[msg.sender];
        balances[msg.sender] = 0;
        msg.sender.transfer(amount);
    }

    function () payable {
        balances[wife] += msg.value / 2;
        balances[husband] += msg.value / 2;
    }
}
```

Here we have a contract that splits all incoming money 50-50 between a husband and wife. As we mentioned earlier, updating a word in the state tree consumes 20,000 gas, so the fallback function far exceeds a transfer's 2,300 gas allocation. Listing 5-11 modifies the withdraw function from Listing 5-7 so that our Marriage contract can use it.

Caution   The code in Listing 5-11 is safe, but you should not use it without reading the next section and understanding the risks of re-entrancy.

Listing 5-11. Allow withdraw to Call Complex Fallback Functions

```
// DO NOT USE WITHOUT UNDERSTANDING RE-ENTRANCY
function withdraw () {
    uint amount = balances[msg.sender];
    balances[msg.sender] = 0;
    bool success = msg.sender.call.value(amount)();
    require(success);
}
```

The *address*.call.value(*amount*)() function is the third way of sending ether we mentioned in the previous section. *address*.call(*data*) can be used to call any external contract function. It can accept two modifiers, .value(*amount*) and .gas(*limit*), to make the external call with the given value and gas. If .gas is omitted as we have done here, the method forwards all gas by default.

Here *address*.call returns a bool indicating whether the external call succeeded. If the transfer fails, the require statement will roll back all state changes.

Calling External Contracts

Passing an external contract enough gas to perform complex actions can be dangerous because you cannot control the actions of the external contract. External contracts can run malicious code to perform re-entrancy attacks or induce race conditions. All calls to unknown external functions should be treated as potential attack vectors.

Re-entrancy Attack

A re-entrancy attack occurs when a call to an external contract triggers a malicious function that reenters the original calling contract. Listing 5-12 creates a bad Roulette contract that can be hacked with a re-entrancy attack.

> **Caution**   Do not use the code in this section. These snippets are all open to re-entrancy attacks. Refer to the code in the "Withdraw Methods" section for safe, usable code.

Listing 5-12. Contracts Vulnerable to Re-entrancy Attacks

```
contract HackableRoulette {
    mapping(address => uint) public balances;

    function betRed () payable {
        bool winner = (randomNumber() % 2 == 0);
        if (winner)
            balances[msg.sender] += msg.value * 2;
    }

    function randomNumber() returns (uint) {
        // we will implement this in a later section
        // for now it returns 0 by default
    }

    function withdraw () {
        uint amount = balances[msg.sender];
        msg.sender.call.value(amount)();
        balances[msg.sender] = 0;
    }
}
```

The only difference between this and the safe Roulette contract is the last two lines of the withdraw function. The transfer occurs before zeroing out the user's balance, and *address*.call.value is used instead of *address*.transfer, so all remaining gas is forwarded.

   This means that a withdrawing contract can reenter the
HackableRoulette contract, and that the withdrawer's balance upon
reentry will still be their full balance. Listing 5-13 takes advantage of
these security holes to write a contract that will drain all ether from the
HackableRoulette.

Listing 5-13. Draining a Contract with a Re-entrancy Attack

```
contract ReentrancyAttack {
    HackableRoulette public roulette;

    function ReentrancyAttack(address rouletteAddress) {
        roulette = HackableRoulette(rouletteAddress);
    }

    function hack () payable {
        // bet on red until the contract wins a bet
        // and has a non-zero balance
        while (roulette.balances(address(this)) == 0)
            roulette.betRed.value(msg.value)();

        roulette.withdraw();
    }

    // fallback called by HackableRoulette.withdraw
    function () payable {
        if (roulette.balance >=
        roulette.balances(address(this)))
            roulette.withdraw();
    }
}
```

This contract is instantiated with the address of the HackableRoulette contract. When the hack function is called, it first places bets until it wins one of the bets. This is necessary because the internal balance on the HackableRoulette contract needs to be nonzero to withdraw ether.

Once the balance is nonzero, we can start the withdraw loop by calling roulette.withdraw(). The roulette's withdraw function then sends ether to the ReentrancyAttack contract, which triggers its fallback function. The fallback function then runs another withdrawal, and because the balance hasn't been zeroed out yet, HackableRoulette allows ReentrancyAttack to withdraw its full balance again. This loop continues until HackableRoulette's contract balance is less than ReentrancyAttack's internal balance, at which point no more ether can be drained.

Note   You can test this attack on your own by using our official GitHub repo. Contracts (https://github.com/k26dr/ethereum-games/blob/master/contracts/ReentrancyAttack.sol), a migration (https://github.com/k26dr/ethereum-games/blob/master/migrations/5_reentrancy_attack.js), and a test file (https://github.com/k26dr/ethereum-games/blob/master/test/reentrancy.js) are all provided. From the project root, run truffle test test/reentrancy.js to watch it in action.

There are two ways to block the attack: zero out the balance before calling the external contract or use msg.transfer to limit the gas provided and prevent re-entrancy. Using both would bring us back to the safe implementation of Listing 5-7. If you still want to be able to execute complex external fallback functions, Listing 5-14 will allow you to do so. You will get a chance to test re-entrancy attacks on your own in Exercise 5-2.

Listing 5-14. Safely Allow Complex Fallback Functions

```
function withdraw () {
    uint amount = balances[msg.sender];
    balances[msg.sender] = 0;
    msg.sender.call.value(amount)();
}
```

EXERCISE 5-2. PREVENTING RE-ENTRANCY

Modify the HackableRoulette contract so that it first reflects the code in Listing 5-7, and then the code in Listing 5-14. Run the re-entrancy test again for each modification and watch the test fail when it attempts to drain the contract's ether.

Race Conditions

Race condition is the general term for the class of bugs that can occur when calling external contracts. A race condition can occur when any unknown state change occurs in an external function call. A re-entrancy attack is one form of race condition. Another form of race condition can occur if two contracts are both modifying the same variable in a third contract. Race conditions that don't involve re-entrancy are rare, and we cover them only if they appear in our games.

Suspendable Contracts

All contracts that either handle large amounts of ether or receive ether for limited durations of time should be suspendable.

If a contract holds a large amount of ether and a critical bug is found, suspending a contract can put it into withdraw-only mode and prevent unsafe external interaction with the contract.

If a contract accepts ether for a limited amount of time as in a token sale, suspending the contract instead of killing it prevents investors from losing their ether if they participate too late. Listing 5-15 contains an example of a suspendable token sale contract.

Listing 5-15. Suspendable Contracts

```solidity
contract TokenSale {
    enum State { Active, Suspended }

    address public owner;
    ERC20 public token;
    State public state;

    function TokenSale(address tokenContractAddress) {
        owner = msg.sender;
        token = ERC20(tokenContractAddress);
        state = State.Active;
    }

    // 1:1 exchange of ETH for token
    function buy() payable {
        require(state == State.Active);
        token.transfer(msg.sender, msg.value);
    }

    function suspend () {
        require(msg.sender == owner);
        state = State.Suspended;
    }

    function activate () {
        require(msg.sender == owner);
        state = State.Active;
    }
```

```
function withdraw() {
    require(msg.sender == owner);
    owner.transfer(address(this).balance);
}
}
```

There is an enumerable in the contract tracking the state. For an investor to buy tokens, the state must be active. At any point, the owner of the contract can suspend the contract and prevent investors from buying tokens. The owner can also reactivate the contract after suspending it. The owner of the contract can withdraw all the ether from the contract at any time, even if the contract is suspended.

When the contract is suspended, it rejects all attempts to send ether to it. This is better than self-destructing the contract. A self-destructed contract is equivalent to a wallet address with no private key. Any ether sent to a self-destructed contract is lost. If an investor accidentally sends ether to a suspended contract, it will reject the transaction and return their ether instead of losing it.

Random-Number Generation

Ethereum is a deterministic environment, so Solidity does not have a built-in source of entropy that can be used to generate random numbers. The closest we can get to a source of entropy is blockhashes. When a block is mined, it produces an unguessable blockhash. We can access the most recent blockhash in our contracts with the `block.blockhash(block.number - 1)` expression. Listing 5-16 demonstrates a random-number generator (RNG) by using `block.blockhash`.

Listing 5-16. Random Numbers from Parent Blockhash

```
function random(uint seed) public view returns (uint) {
    return uint(
        keccak256(block.blockhash(block.number-1), seed)
    );
}
```

This function hashes the parent blockhash with a user-generated seed and then takes the integer representation of the bytes. Changing the seed will change the output. This gives a number between 0 and 2^{256} that can be used with a modulus to get a smaller range of numbers:

```
// Random number from 0-99
random(0x7543def) % 100;
```

Although the blockhash is guaranteed to be lower than the block difficulty, the exact number is unknown until the block is mined. Unfortunately, the blockhash of the current block is unavailable until after the block is mined, so we have to use the blockhash from the parent block. This means that the random number can be guessed by anyone who has access to the parent blockhash and seed. Additionally, only the 256 most recent blockhashes are available, and attempting to call `block.blockhash` for a block older than that will return 0x0.

As a simple attack, the random number can be guessed by an attacker by copying and pasting our `random` function into their contract and making sure it gets mined in the same block as a transaction that uses our random function. This way, the parent blockhash will be the same, and the only unknown is the seed. The seed must come from user input in the transaction or from a deterministic source in the contract, either of which can be known beforehand.

The only way to maintain the randomness of the source is to use a two-transaction system. The first transaction locks in a future block number as the source of entropy. After that selected block has been mined, the second transaction uses that block's blockhash as the source of entropy to run its logic.

The two-transaction RNG system is fairly secure, if slow, but it can still be slightly manipulated by a miner. Let's say our RNG is being used to determine the winner of a lottery in which the miner is a participant. When the miner generates a valid blockhash, they can choose to discard the hash and continue mining if the random number it generates does not result in them winning the lottery. This allows them to increase their chance of winning by an amount proportional to their hashpower on the network.

Although this is an issue in theory, there have been no documented cases of this attack. That being said, a sufficiently large jackpot that far exceeds the block reward would likely lead a miner to attempt this attack.

Knowing all these flaws, the conclusion is that we should not rely on our simple RNG to secure large amounts of ether. If you need to secure a large amount of ether with a random number, a superior but far more complex method of generating random numbers through a lottery is covered in Chapter 8.

Issues with Integers

Using integer data types in Solidity without safety checks can lead to buggy code. The two classes of errors we will look at are underflow/overflow errors and errors due to a lack of decimal support in the language.

Underflow/Overflow

Solidity does not protect against overflow and underflow errors. An overflow occurs when the value of an integer type exceeds its maximum value. An underflow occurs when the value goes below the minimum value.

The min value for a uint is 0. The max value is $2b - 1$, where b is the length of the data type in bits. So a uint8 has a max value $28 - 1 = 255$, while a uint, which is 256 bytes long, has a max value of $2256 - 1$.

The min value for an int is $2b - 1$, and the max value is $2b - 1 - 1$. For int8, the min value would be –128, and the max value would be 127.

When an integer overflows, it goes back down to its minimum value. When an integer underflows, it goes up to its maximum value.

All the examples in Listing 5-17 cause overflow or underflow.

Listing 5-17. Integer Underflow/Overflow

```
uint a = 5;
a -= 6; // 2²⁵⁶ -1
a += 1; // 0

int8 b = 64;
b *= 3; // -64

// this loop never ends because i overflows
uint[300] numbers;
uint sum = 0;
for (uint8 i=0; i < numbers.length; i++)
    sum += numbers[i];
```

To prevent under- and overflow, most developers use a standard contract called SafeMath. The SafeMath contract checks for over- and underflow conditions and throws an error if it recognizes one. The SafeMath contract is reproduced in Listing 5-18 if you wish to use it.

Listing 5-18. SafeMath to Protect Against Under- and Overflow

```
contract SafeMath {
    function safeMul(uint a, uint b) internal pure returns
    (uint) {
        uint c = a * b;
        assert(a == 0 || c / a == b);
        return c;
    }

    function safeDiv(uint a, uint b) internal pure returns
    (uint) {
        assert(b > 0);
        uint c = a / b;
        assert(a == b * c + a % b);
        return c;
    }

    function safeSub(uint a, uint b) internal pure returns
    (uint) {
        assert(b <= a);
        return a - b;
    }

    function safeAdd(uint a, uint b) internal pure returns
    (uint) {
        uint c = a + b;
        assert(c>=a && c>=b);
        return c;
    }
}
```

Truncated Division

Solidity does not support decimal numbers, so integers must be used to approximate decimal operations. We covered simulating decimal precision in Listing 3-32. Anytime a division operation occurs, there is the possibility of losing precision to truncation. *Truncation* in integer division occurs when two numbers don't divide evenly and the decimal digits get dropped. So 11 / 2 would get truncated to 5 in Solidity.

It is most important to keep this in mind when tracking assets for which the smallest subdivision of the asset has significant value. With ether, losing track of 1 or 2 wei is not a big deal.

Now let's say we're trading shares of Google (GOOG), which can't be subdivided and are worth $1,000 each. If we write a contract that splits a holding between two people, as in Listing 5-19, we can lose a stock to truncation.

Listing 5-19. Losing Assets to Truncation

```
// WARNING: This contract will not compile without
// defining a Stock contract
contract MarriageInvestment {
    address wife = address(0); // dummy address
    address husband = address(1); // dummy address
    Stock GOOG = Stock(address(2)); // dummy contract

    function split () public {
        uint amount = GOOG.balanceOf(address(this));
        uint each = amount / 2;
        GOOG.transfer(husband, each);
        GOOG.transfer(wife, each);
    }
}
```

This contract takes a stock holding and divides it between a husband and wife. Let's say the holding for the couple is three shares. When attempting to split the holding between the couple, each person would get one share. The last remaining share is inaccessible because 1 / 2 = 0!

This can be fixed by transferring any remaining shares to one of the participants (Listing 5-20).

Listing 5-20. Preventing Asset Loss from Integer Truncation

```
function split () public {
    uint amount = GOOG.balanceOf(address(this));
    uint each = amount / 2;
    uint remainder = amount % 2;
    GOOG.transfer(husband, each + remainder);
    GOOG.transfer(wife, each);
}
```

Functions Are Public by Default

Functions without a visibility modifier in Solidity are public by default. As we mentioned in Chapter 4, best practice is to explicitly specify a visibility modifier on each function. As of version 0.4.17, the compiler will include a warning if a function has no visibility modifier specified. You should be treating warnings like errors and updating code until all compiler warnings are fixed.

Failing to mark a function that is supposed to be private with an appropriate visibility modifier was the source of the Parity multi-sig hack. A function that was supposed to be internal was unmarked and got used to take control of the wallet.

Use msg.sender Instead of tx.origin

The property tx.origin is an alternative available to msg.sender in contract functions. Whereas msg.sender points to the most recent contract or wallet address that called the particular function, tx.origin points to the wallet address that signed the originating transaction. The best use for tx.origin is to not use it. In almost all situations, msg.sender is the appropriate property to use.

Using msg.sender allows the contract to modify internal contract state (such as balances) associated with an address on the sender's behalf. Because the sender must directly call the contract method, it is considered safe to use.

Using tx.origin in your contracts exposes your users to forwarding attacks. Let's create a function that uses tx.origin for authorization and see how it can be hacked (see Listing 5-21).

Caution   Code in this section can be hacked. Do not use it in your contracts.

Listing 5-21. Bad Authorization with tx.origin

```
// DO NOT USE: BAD CODE
function transferTo(address dest) {
    require(tx.origin == owner);
    dest.transfer(address(this).balance);
}
```

This function allows the owner of the contract to send the balance of the contract to any destination address. A hacker can take advantage of that with a forwarding contract, as in Listing 5-22.

Listing 5-22. Forwarding Attack on tx.origin Authorization

```
contract ForwardingAttack {
    HackableTransfer hackable;
    address attacker;

    function ForwardingAttack (address _hackable) public {
        hackable = HackableTransfer(_hackable);
        attacker = msg.sender;
    }

    function () payable public {
        hackable.transferTo(attacker);
    }
}
```

The hack works as follows. The attacker convinces you to send ether to the address of the attacking contract by pretending to be a regular wallet address and requesting payment for a service. When you send the ether, the fallback function on the attacking contract calls the transferTo function in the vulnerable contract and attempts to transfer the vulnerable contract's balance to the attacker's wallet address. Because the transaction originated with your wallet address, the authorization passes, and the attacker transfers all your ether in the vulnerable contract to their wallet address.

To prevent the attack, simply change tx.origin to msg.sender, as shown in Listing 5-23.

Listing 5-23. Protecting Against Forwarding Attacks

```
// SAFE CODE
function transferTo(address dest) {
    require(msg.sender == owner);
    dest.transfer(address(this).balance);
}
```

Everything Can Be Front-Run

Transactions are broadcast to the whole network and are generally visible to all nodes before being included in a block. When transactions are included in a block, they are included in order of transaction fee. This opens up the opportunity for front running.

Front running is the process of viewing a transaction and taking advantage of its contents to send a transaction of your own. If your transaction clears before the original transaction, you have *front-run* it. Because all transactions are publicly visible and there is no global mechanism forcing a transaction order, all orders can be front-run.

In practice, this is how it would work. Let's say someone has set up a prize puzzle, where the winning answer unlocks a reward of 5 ether. Because all computation in Ethereum is deterministic, it can be determined beforehand whether a given answer will unlock the prize. An attacker scans all transactions going into a contract, and if he detects a winning answer, he sends a transaction copying the winning answer but sets his gas price much higher than the original winner. Because transactions are processed in order of gas price, the attacker's answer will be processed first, and the attacker will win the prize.

Protections against front running are different for each contract. For the prize contract, we could institute a guessing period and publish the answer after the guessing period has concluded so that new answers can't claim the prize. As we go through the games in the latter half of the book, we will tackle the front-running problem in different ways.

Previous Hacks and Attacks

Ethereum smart contracts have suffered a number of fatal bugs that have been exploited in the past. This section walks through the major incidents and discusses the lessons learned from each incident.

The DAO

The DAO attack is the most infamous of all the Ethereum hacks and resulted in a loss of 3.5 million ether before a hard fork rolled back the hack. The attack was so large that the Ethereum Foundation decided to hard-fork to roll back the transaction that created the hack and return the DAO funds to investors. This highly contentious fork eventually led to the split between Ethereum Classic, which did not fork, and the main Ethereum chain, which did fork.

The DAO attack was a complex re-entrancy attack. The vulnerable code is reproduced in Listing 5-24. The two lines that permit the re-entrancy are in bold. As you can see, the balance is being zeroed out after the transfer to the external contract.

Listing 5-24. DAO Vulnerability

```
    // This is the end of the splitDAO function
    Transfer(msg.sender, 0, balances[msg.sender]);
    withdrawRewardFor(msg.sender);
    totalSupply -= balances[msg.sender];
    balances[msg.sender] = 0;
    paidOut[msg.sender] = 0;
    return true;
}
```

The withdrawRewardFor function calls a payOut function that sends ether to an external address in Listing 5-25.

Listing 5-25. Payout Function in the DAO

```
function payOut(address _recipient, uint _amount) returns
(bool) {
    if (msg.sender != owner || msg.value > 0
        || (payOwnerOnly && _recipient != owner))
```

```
        throw;
    if (_recipient.call.value(_amount)()) {
        PayOut(_recipient, _amount);
        return true;
    } else {
        return false;
    }
}
```

The bolded portion is where the external call occurs. It uses the unsafe *address*.call.value method to send ether and forward all gas, so the attacker was able to use this to set up a contract with a fallback function and repeat the withdraw loop to drain the contract. We saw code to perform this attack in the "Re-entrancy Attack" section.

In this case, the recipient contract had a restriction that it had to be a child DAO. Because of internal rules, the funds were locked for seven days before they could be used:

```
// The minimum debate period that a split proposal can have
uint constant minSplitDebatePeriod = 1 weeks;
```

This holding period is what allowed the hard fork to execute safely. If the funds had been withdrawn immediately, they could have been moved to exchanges and traded, at which point rolling back the hack would have been infeasible, because regular people holding ether would have been affected as well.

Parity Multi-Sig

The Parity multi-sig wallet was a smart contract built into the Parity software that required multiple keys to sign off on any spending of funds. Many ICO startups were using it to secure their funds. It had an insecure fallback function that allowed attackers to drain 150,000 ether in total from multiple contracts.

The culprit was a function in a library that should have been inaccessible to the public (Listing 5-26).

Listing 5-26. Parity Multi-sig Wallet Vulnerability

```
function initWallet(address[] _owners, uint _required, uint
_daylimit) {
    initDaylimit(_daylimit);
    initMultiowned(_owners, _required);
}
```

This function initializes a multi-sig wallet with multiple owners. It should be called only when the contract is initialized. It allows anybody with access to the function to reset the contract and declare new owners. Library functions are usually inaccessible via the ABI, but this contract contained an overly permissive fallback function reproduced in Listing 5-27 for executing undeclared functions.

Listing 5-27. Overly Permissive Fallback Function

```
function () payable {
    // just being sent some cash?
    if (msg.value > 0)
      Deposit(msg.sender, msg.value);
    else if (msg.data.length > 0)
      _walletLibrary.delegatecall(msg.data);
}
```

The fallback function executes when any unmatched function name is called. The delegatecall function can be used to forward function calls onto a different library or contract. In this case, any unmatched function was being forwarded to a library that contained the initWallet function. The attacker was able to call that function and use it to make himself the owner, and then drain the funds.

The fix to this one is simple. Never use `.delegatecall`. It is dangerous and can easily lead to security holes. You should be explicitly stating any functions you want forwarded.

Coindash

The Coindash hack wasn't actually a smart contract vulnerability; it was an old-fashioned web hack. During Coindash's ICO, a hacker replaced the Ethereum address on the Coindash ICO with their own address. This led investors to send 30,000 ether to the attacker's address instead of the Coindash ICO contract.

Governmental

Governmental's contract wasn't hacked, but it suffered from a subtle bug that made the contract's prize allocation inaccessible for a few months. Governmental was a pyramid scheme contract. We discuss more about the details of their contract in Chapter 7, but the basics involved one player being able to capture a large prize at the end.

The payout code looked like Listing 5-28.

Listing 5-28. Governmental Payout Code

```
// Sends all contract money to the last creditor
creditorAddresses[creditorAddresses.length -
1].send(profitFromCrash);
corruptElite.send(this.balance);

// Reset contract state
lastCreditorPayedOut = 0;
lastTimeOfNewCredit = block.timestamp;
profitFromCrash = 0;
```

```
creditorAddresses = new address[](0);
creditorAmounts = new uint[](0);
round += 1;
return false;
```

The two lines in bold required updating a large amount of storage in the state tree. Hundreds of people had participated in the game, so hundreds of addresses and amounts had to be set to zero. The gas fee for this transaction was so high that it exceeded the block gas limit at the time, and the payout couldn't be claimed by the winner. The winner had to wait for the block gas limit to increase before claiming the reward.

Summary

This chapter covered the ins and outs of writing secure contracts with Solidity. You now know how to send, store, and withdraw ether safely with smart contracts, how to create random numbers, and the many potential security pitfalls to watch out for during development. You are now ready to progress to the projects. Before we get to that, however, we are going to take a slight detour away from code to discuss the economics and incentives behind blockchains.

CHAPTER 6

Crypto-economics and Game Theory

Crypto-economics is the name given to the emerging study of incentives, economics, and game theory associated with maintaining a blockchain. If economics can be simplified as the study of incentives, *crypto-economics* is the study of blockchain-related incentives. In this chapter, we cover block production methods, blockchain security, consensus, the importance of good incentives, and the most common attack vectors on a typical blockchain.

Securing the Blockchain

Currently, the majority of successful blockchains are secured by *hashpower*: the computing power behind proof-of-work (PoW) mining. Other blockchains have begun experimenting with proof-of-stake (PoS) and proof-of-authority (PoA), two methods for creating security in the system. Ethereum's researchers have stated that the network will soon be switching to proof-of-stake, so that will be of special interest to us.

© Kedar Iyer and Chris Dannen 2018
K. Iyer and C. Dannen, *Building Games with Ethereum Smart Contracts*,
https://doi.org/10.1007/978-1-4842-3492-1_6

Proof-of-Work

The creation of the proof-of-work methodology was one of the chief enabling innovations for Bitcoin. Ethereum has committed to using proof-of-work for the first three years of its existence so far, after which it plans to use proof-of-stake. We discussed proof-of-work mining briefly in Chapter 1.

Proof-of-work was first proposed in a 1992 paper as an antispam measure. It was proposed again separately as a measure to prevent DDoS attacks. Neither was particularly successful, but it paved the way for its use in cryptocurrencies.

Bitcoin uses SHA-256 hashing in its proof-of-work algorithm. Miners hash the block header repeatedly with SHA-256, using the *nonce* and *timestamp* fields to create new inputs. Miners that generate a hash lower than the 32-byte network difficulty propagate their blocks to the network. As a reward for their hashpower, miners can include a *coinbase* transaction rewarding themselves with new bitcoin.

Many variants of the proof-of-work algorithm have been designed to remedy SHA-256's shortcomings. The simplicity of the SHA-256 algorithm makes it easy to mine with application-specific integrated circuits (ASICs). Litecoin uses Scrypt, which was intended to be memory-intensive, but an ASIC was created for it anyway. Monero uses CryptoNight, which has successfully utilized specialized system calls to make traditional CPU mining the most effective method.

Ethereum uses Ethash, a custom algorithm that, true to its design, has remained the most successful method to mine with graphics processing units (GPUs). Ethash requires repetitive reads from a directed acyclic graph (DAG) stored in memory. The DAG is greater than 1GB in size, so ASICs, which generally contain very little memory, are not feasible for mining.

If you want to know the exact details of the Ethash algorithm, check out the Ethash wiki (https://github.com/ethereum/wiki/wiki/Ethash). For test mining code, you can generate the current DAG with the following:

```
geth makedag
```

Proof-of-work mining secures the blockchain by forcing any attacker who wishes to take over the network to control 51% of the hashpower (see "51% Attacks"). Block rewards and transaction fees incentivize miners to mine blocks. The network difficulty is adjusted regularly to maintain a target mean block time. The target mean block time of the Ethereum network is currently around 20 seconds.

This number is slowly creeping upward due to the "difficulty bomb" in Ethereum's code, which slowly raises the mean block time. The motive behind this is to force Ethereum to switch to proof-of-stake when block times get too large and place a cap on the creation of new ether from block rewards. After proof-of-stake is introduced, the block reward will probably be decreased or may even go to zero.

Proof-of-Stake

The details of Ethereum's proof-of-stake implementation are still being hashed out, with no strict timetable for completion. There are multiple types of proof-of-stake implementations, each with its own method of securing the blockchain. Ethereum's proof-of-stake system is called *Casper* and allows users to confirm blocks by betting on the probability of their approval by the network.

The first proof-of-stake coin was Peercoin, which uses the principle of coin-age to secure blocks and mint new supply. More recently, Steemit and EOS use Delegated Proof of Stake (DPOS). DPOS requires users to vote in a series of block producers who are then authorized to produce blocks. If Casper is analogous to a pure democracy, DPOS is more of a representative democracy.

Ethereum plans to institute Casper in the near future.

Proof-of-Authority

A *proof-of-authority* blockchain is similar to a permissioned blockchain. Only nodes with authorized keys can publish blocks, so it is not actually a decentralized system. Proof-of-authority blockchains can produce blocks at a much faster rate than decentralized networks because there is no need for the network to come to consensus or mine blocks.

The Ropsten and Kovan testnets for Ethereum are proof-of-authority chains. Test ether is worthless, so block rewards and transaction fees essentially don't exist. This means there is no incentive to mine blocks or prevent transaction spamming. The standard block production process becomes too easy to attack (see "Testnet Attacks and Issues"), so proof-of-authority must be used for testnets instead.

Forming Consensus

Consensus is the process through which nodes decide whether to add a block to the blockchain. Consensus is formed through a shared set of rules. All nodes on a network must operate by a compatible set of rules if they wish to reach a common consensus. Consensus rules are referred to as *block validation rules* by some blockchains because they are used to determine whether a node will accept a block into its local copy of the blockchain.

In Ethereum, the consensus rules are encoded in the execution of the Ethereum Virtual Machine (EVM) and the Merkle root of the state tree. Each node executes the transactions in a block in order. Each transaction is a series of EVM `opcodes` executed in sequence. Assuming that nodes have the same rules for EVM execution, they will arrive at the same final state.

A *fork* occurs when a set of nodes on a network adopt a different set of consensus rules. A *soft fork* occurs when the new rules are a subset of the old rules. Only miners have to update their software to the new rules because nodes using the old version will still validate blocks produced by the new rules.

A *hard fork* occurs when the new rules are not a subset of the new rules. Everyone must update their software in a hard fork. Nodes that refuse to update their software in a hard fork will diverge from the nodes that update. This is how Ethereum Classic was formed. Some nodes refused to update their software to accommodate the DAO fork.

Transaction Fees

Transaction fees secure the network by preventing malicious actors from spamming the network. The use of transaction fees creates a marketplace for access to the network and prioritizes access for those who find it most valuable (those who are willing to pay the highest fees).

In many blockchains, the transaction fee is the only form of payment that must be denominated in the network's native currency. This is why you will sometimes hear it mentioned that ether derives its value from the net present value (NPV) of future transaction fees, similar to the way a stock derives its value from the NPV of future dividends. However, because the value produced by the transaction fees give ether a further utility as a programmable currency, it might be more accurate to say that the NPV of future transaction fees acts as a floor for the price of ether.

Incentives

Good incentive mechanisms are the foundation of a secure blockchain. When evaluating a new blockchain technology, the first question you should be asking yourself is, "What sort of behaviors does this blockchain incentivize?" You must assume that users in a blockchain will always maximize their own self-interest. The anonymity and potential for large profits make it too easy to take advantage of poor design.

Blockchains are successful because they can operate smoothly under any conditions, including when under attack. We will see what happens to a blockchain with poorly designed incentives in the "Testnet Attacks and Issues" section.

Let's walk through some of the incentive systems in place for Ethereum and describe how they contribute to securing the network:

- *Block rewards*: Miners receive a block reward when they successfully mine a block, so they are willing to invest in infrastructure to generate hashpower for the network. Greater hashpower secures the network by making it difficult for a single entity to take over the network with a 51% attack.

- *Network difficulty*: The network difficulty increases as the hashpower of the network increases, creating an arms race between miners to generate the most hashpower possible. Miners are incentivized to invest in greater hashpower until their economic profit reaches zero.

- *Transaction fees*: Prevent spammers from clogging up the network with useless transactions.

- *Consensus rules*: Decentralize power in the network by giving each node an equal say in which blocks get accepted. Miners don't waste valuable hashpower producing malicious blocks because they will be rejected by the network.

Attack Vectors

No set of incentives is perfect. Every blockchain will have a series of attack vectors that can be used to exploit the system. The goal of a well-designed system is to make exploiting the available attack vectors as difficult as possible. Let's look at some basic attack vectors that can be used to attack the Ethereum network.

51% Attacks

The Ethereum mining system is designed to be secure so long as no one entity controls over half the hashpower. A single entity that controls over half the hashpower can destroy faith in the network by conducting a 51% attack.

There can be only one main chain when multiple versions of the chain head exist. The rule for determining which is the main chain is simple: the longest chain is the main chain. The most secure chain is the one with the most hashpower on it, and the longest chain will be the one with the most hashpower. Furthermore, the rule for determining the main chain must be simple enough for all nodes to come to the same consensus in a decentralized fashion.

The attack would be conducted as follows: the attacker mines blocks on the network but doesn't broadcast them, letting a number of them accumulate locally. Because the attacker controls more than half the hashpower, their local chain will be longer than the main chain. After a significant number of blocks have passed—say, a day's worth of blocks—the attacker broadcasts their blocks all at once, invalidating any transactions that occurred in the last day.

Merchants or any sellers of goods that accepted payments in ether would have to track down their customers and demand repayment or return of the good. Doing this repeatedly would destroy faith in the network. As of now, this attack is highly theoretical for the larger blockchains. The amount of capital required to amass 51% of the hashpower is prohibitively high to just turn around and destroy the network that gives the equipment value. It would take a well-funded malicious actor with a seriously good reason to take down the network to perform a 51% attack on one of the larger chains like Bitcoin or Ethereum. No one has ever successfully pulled off the attack, so it would be a big gamble to attempt it.

Network Spamming

We mentioned earlier that transaction fees prevent spammers from clogging up the network with useless transactions. That was a bit of a misrepresentation. Transaction fees actually just make spamming the network a very expensive affair that serves mainly to fill blocks and raise transaction fees for the remainder of the network.

Network spamming has been used most effectively in Ethereum when targeting specific bugs in the EVM. In September 2016, a network spam attack targeting the EXTCODESIZE opcode increased block validation times to 60 seconds.[1] The EXTCODESIZE opcode performs a disk read to get the size of a contract's code in the state tree. This opcode was underpriced with a gas fee of 20 gas, so calling it repeatedly forced each block validation to perform about 50,000 disk reads and slowed down the whole network.[2] The problem was eventually fixed in EIP 150 (Ethereum Improvement Proposal 150) by increasing the gas cost for the opcode to 700.[3]

Spam attacks have proven to be much more successful on the Ethereum testnets where transaction fees are paid in the valueless test ether. We discuss those in the "Testnet Attacks and Issues" section.

---

[1]Ethereum Blog, "Transaction Spam Attacks: Next Steps", https://blog. ethereum.org/2016/09/22/transaction-spam-attack-next-steps/

[2]"EVM 1.0 gas costs", https://docs.google.com/spreadsheets/d/1m89CVujr Qe5LAFJ8-YAUCcNK950dUzMQPMJBxRtGCqs/edit#gid=0

[3]Github, "Ethereum Improvement Proposal 150", https://github.com/ethereum/ EIPs/blob/master/EIPS/eip-150.md

Breaking Cryptography

The most effective way to kill a blockchain would be to break one of the cryptographic algorithms used by the network. Ethereum's proof-of-work algorithm, Ethash, uses Keccack256 as a hashing algorithm and the Secp256k1 elliptic curve to generate public and private keys. Breaking either of these would cause an irredeemable loss of confidence in the system. Thankfully, breaking these algorithms is no easy task.

Both algorithms use one-way functions to create security. A one-way function is easy to compute in one direction, but hard to compute in the other. Given a message, it is easy to compute the Keccak256 hash of the message. Given the hash, it is nearly impossible to compute the message.

Hash functions are used extensively in Ethereum smart contracts to obscure information. As we've seen, Keccak256 is used not only in Ethash, but also as an opcode in the EVM, as an instruction in Solidity, as well as in address, transaction, and block hashing, in the ABI, and in the Merkle Patricia trie.

When we do prize puzzles later, we will use hashes to obscure the answer. There are simple ways to attack hash functions. The most basic is a dictionary attack. Keep a large key/value database mapping hashes of common words and bit sequences to their hashes. Then when you encounter a hash, run it through the database and see whether it matches any of your common sequences.

To avoid having your hash cracked by a dictionary attack, use a salt. A *salt* is a random sequence you stick in front of every word you hash to make the output unique enough that it won't show up in a database of common hashes. If you salt your hashes properly, the only way to attack them is by trying random sequences and hashing them until you get a match. Doing so is so expensive that not even a supercomputer should be able to crack a standard Keccak256 hash.

The same idea goes for public-private keys. Public keys are generated from private keys by using elliptic curves. The details are beyond the scope of this book, but a simple primer is available at `https://arstechnica.com/information-technology/2013/10/a-relatively-easy-to-understand-primer-on-elliptic-curve-cryptography/` I if you're interested. Determining the private key from the public key is even harder than breaking the Keccak256 hash. But anybody who can do so would be able to take control of any address on the network and their corresponding ether.

Replay Attacks

Replay attacks occur only during hard forks. They were a major issue during the split between Ethereum and Ethereum Classic. Many people who sent a transaction on Ethereum after the hard fork had their transactions replayed on the Ethereum Classic chain.

During a fork, all users have the same balance on both forks. This meant that anyone with an Ethereum balance at the time of the fork had an equivalent Ethereum Classic balance as well. Unfortunately, because the chains used the exact same transaction logic, a transaction on Ethereum was also valid on Ethereum Classic.

Balances are generally protected by a user's private key; the user has to sign a transaction with their private key to send their ether. Right after the fork, though, users were using the same private keys for both Ethereum and Ethereum Classic, and a signed transaction on Ethereum was valid on Ethereum Classic as well. Attackers took advantage by taking signed transactions broadcast on the Ethereum network and broadcasting them to the Ethereum Classic network too. This meant anyone sending their Ethereum was unknowingly sending the recipient their Ethereum Classic also.

The strange part of replay attacks is that the attackers themselves rarely benefit from the attack. Only the recipients of the transaction benefit, and most recipients aren't malicious or savvy enough to conduct the attack. However, anybody can carry out the attack on behalf of the recipient, so malicious actors were replaying transactions in order to destabilize Ethereum.

Protecting against replay attacks is simple. EIP 155 (`https://github.com/ethereum/EIPs/blob/master/EIPS/eip-155.md`) fixed the issue by adding a chain ID field to the transaction. Ethereum has chain ID 1, and Ethereum Classic has chain ID 61. If the chain ID of the transaction doesn't match the chain ID of the network client, the client rejects the transaction.

Testnet Attacks and Issues

Keeping a proof-of-work testnet up and running has proven to be a difficult challenge for Ethereum. Because testnet ether has no value, miners have no incentive to mine the chain, so 51% attacks and network spam attacks that would ordinarily be prohibitively expensive to carry out become trivial. Each of the proof-of-work testnets used in the past by Ethereum have been taken down by attackers.

The first Ethereum release was the Olympic testnet. It occasionally came under spam attack—but nothing serious. The main issue with the testnet came when the initial upgrade to the Frontier mainnet took place. Because Frontier didn't have replay protection, anybody reusing keys/addresses between Olympic and Frontier could have their test Olympic transactions replayed on the Frontier mainnet. Users were warned to use different keys for the new Frontier mainnet in order to avoid this problem.

The next official Ethereum testnet was Morden. Morden uses the account nonce to implement replay protection. It set the starting nonce of every account on the network to 2**20 to prevent transactions from being replayed on the mainnet. Unfortunately, when EIP 161 (`https://github.com/ethereum/EIPs/blob/master/EIPS/eip-161.md`) implemented a change to the nonce creation code, a Morden-specific difference in the

Parity and geth implementations led to a consensus split (a fork) between the two clients. At this point, it was decided to retire the Morden testnet and replace it with the new Ropsten testnet.

Ropsten implemented EIP 155 (`https://github.com/ethereum/EIPs/blob/master/EIPS/eip-155.md`) replay protection to prevent transactions from being replayed on the mainnet. The network difficulty still remained low, though, so a small amount of hashpower was enough to control the network.

A year into Ropsten's existence, a malicious user took over the network hashpower and began inflating the block size. Every time a block is mined, the miner can propose a block gas limit increase of 1/1024 of the current block gas limit. The malicious miner repeatedly did this and filled the blocks with large spam transactions that took a long time to import and validate. The blocks became so large and slow that syncing with the network became impossible, and Ropsten had to be temporarily retired.

Ropsten was replaced by Rinkeby, a proof-of-authority testnet. Proof-of-authority whitelists a series of authorities to produce blocks. Rinkeby produces blocks every 15 seconds. It isn't as realistic as a mined testnet in which block production time is variable, but it is impervious to attacks by miners and spammers.

A revival of the Ropsten testnet was eventually created using a donation of GPU hashpower. The hashpower was used to mine a new longest chain from before the spam attack. Because the longest chain is the main chain, this new longest chain allowed clients to drop the spam blocks. All nonspam transactions were then replayed on the revival chain.

Summary

Proof-of-work, proof-of-stake, and proof-of-authority are the three methods used for securing blockchains in the Ethereum ecosystem. Proof-of-work is the currently used security method. Proof-of-stake will replace proof-of-work in an upcoming Ethereum hard fork with the Casper protocol. Proof-of-authority is used in the Ethereum testnets.

In addition to proof-of-work hashpower, nodes use consensus rules to secure the network. Nodes individually apply their software-encoded consensus rules to a block and its transactions and decide whether to accept the block. In the case of multiple competing blocks or chains, the longest chain is the main chain. All nodes in a network must use the exact same consensus rules to validate blocks. If a subset of the network decides to use a different set of rules, a fork occurs and the chains split.

Blockchains use incentives and market mechanisms to induce desired behavior. Designing proper incentive structures is the key to building a successful blockchain. Block rewards, transaction fees, and network difficulty adjustments are all examples of incentives used by Ethereum to secure the blockchain and promote beneficial behavior.

Incentive systems are never perfect, though, and there will always be attack vectors. Ethereum in particular has in the past been shown to be vulnerable to spam attacks targeted at specific bugs in the platform and replay attacks. Fifty-one percent attacks and cryptographic attacks, while theoretically possible, have not been used against the Ethereum mainnet so far.

Testnets are another story. Because proof-of-work testnet block rewards and transaction fees are valueless, it is cheap to both spam the network and control the hashpower and block production. The testnet we use in this book, Rinkeby, is a proof-of-authority blockchain in which only whitelisted addresses can produce blocks.

In the preceding four chapters, we covered the basics of the Solidity language, best security practices for Solidity, and the basics of how a blockchain operates. With this knowledge, you are ready to build your first game. Let's get started with some simple Ethereum pyramid schemes.

CHAPTER 7

Ponzis and Pyramids

This is the first of the project and game chapters that will take us through the remainder of the book. The first six chapters covered the basics of Ethereum and Solidity. We will now move away from theory and dive in to practical examples of Solidity code. Admittedly, Ponzi schemes do not seem at first glance to be the most practical of examples. Surprisingly, though, some of the first interactive smart contracts released on Ethereum were verifiable Ponzi schemes. In this chapter, we will first write a simple Ponzi contract and then explore examples that were deployed on the Ethereum mainnet.

Schemes: Ponzi vs. Pyramid

In a *pyramid scheme*, participants generate income both by selling a product and recruiting new members to participate in the scheme. Members usually get a cut of the sales revenue of any of the members they recruit. A pyramid scheme is distinguished from its legal brother, multilevel marketing, by the source and distribution of returns. If the majority of returns are from sales, it's multilevel marketing. If the majority of returns are from recruiting, it's a pyramid scheme.

In a *Ponzi scheme*, investors think they're buying a security or investing in a real company that produces returns to its investors. In reality, the money generated from new investment is used to pay off old investors. Ponzi schemes can last for years before falling apart dramatically. These schemes are named for their originator, Charles Ponzi, who famously ran

© Kedar Iyer and Chris Dannen 2018
K. Iyer and C. Dannen, *Building Games with Ethereum Smart Contracts*,
https://doi.org/10.1007/978-1-4842-3492-1_7

such a scheme in the 1920s. But the most famous Ponzi to today's readers is the one run by Bernie Madoff, who took in $20 billion in investments over a span of 48 years and used the continued investment to convince investors their holdings were worth $65 billion.[1]

Pyramid schemes are generally easy to identify because members must recruit additional members to generate any sort of meaningful income. Additionally the "suckers" are a part of the scheme and can see how the company operates. In a Ponzi, the "suckers" are on the outside and don't have any knowledge of the internal workings of the company, so they can last much longer without being discovered.

The terms *pyramid scheme* and *Ponzi scheme* are often used interchangeably, despite meaning different things. As you'll see, the majority of deployed Ethereum schemes are Ponzis, but their creators tend to refer to them as pyramids anyway.

Verifiably Corrupt

Is a Ponzi scheme better if it's verifiably corrupt? So far, the answer from the Ethereum community has been a resounding yes. There was an unnatural level of excitement over Ponzi and pyramid schemes that could be deterministically coded to rip off their users in the early days of Ethereum. Let's write our own simple one before looking at existing ones on the blockchain.

Note   All the code for this chapter is available in our GitHub repo at `https://github.com/k26dr/ethereum-games/blob/` `master/contracts/PonzisAndPyramids.sol`.

---

[1]CNN Money, "Five Things You Didn't Know About Bernie Madoff's Epic Scam," `http://money.cnn.com/2013/12/10/news/companies/bernard-madoff-ponzi/` `index.html`, 2013.

Simple Ponzi

The simplest version of a Ponzi involves taking the money sent by the current investor and transferring it to the previous investor. As long as each investment is larger than the previous one, every investor except the last will get a return on their investment. Let's code this into a contract (Listing 7-1).

Listing 7-1. A Simple Ponzi Scheme

```
contract SimplePonzi {
    address public currentInvestor;
    uint public currentInvestment = 0;

    function () payable public {
        // new investments must be 10% greater than current
        uint minimumInvestment = currentInvestment * 11/10;
        require(msg.value > minimumInvestment);

        // document new investor
        address previousInvestor = currentInvestor;
        currentInvestor = msg.sender;
        currentInvestment = msg.value;

        // payout previous investor
        previousInvestor.send(msg.value);
    }
}
```

Let's walk through the contract in detail a couple of lines at a time, starting with the variables in Listing 7-2.

Listing 7-2. A Simple Ponzi: Variables

```
address public currentInvestor;
uint public currentInvestment = 0;

function () payable public {
```

The contract has two variables: currentInvestor and
currentInvestment. The variable currentInvestor is the address of
the most recent investor in the contract. This address is the only one
that hasn't received a return on their investment, and if no one ever
tops their bid, they will be the one to lose their investment. The variable
currentInvestment is the amount of the investment they stand to lose.

This contract has a single function, the fallback function in Listing 7-3
that can be executed by sending ether directly to the deployed contract's
address.

Listing 7-3. A Simple Ponzi: Minimum Investment

```
uint minimumInvestment = currentInvestment * 11/10;
require(msg.value > minimumInvestment);
```

Any new investment must be at least 10% greater than the current
investment or it will be rejected. Our investors are expecting a juicy return,
and your shenanigans are not welcome here. To calculate the minimum
investment, we need to multiply by 1.1. Unfortunately, we cannot use
decimals in Solidity, so we multiply by 11 and then divide by 10 to achieve
the same effect (Listing 7-4).

Listing 7-4. A Simple Ponzi: Onboarding the New Sucker

```
address previousInvestor = currentInvestor;
currentInvestor = msg.sender;
currentInvestment = msg.value;
```

We keep a reference to the previous investor so we can pay him out with the new investment:

```
previousInvestor.send(msg.value);
```

The new investment is sent directly to the previous investor. No ether is ever actually held in the contract for insignificant things like company development.

An important note: we use `.send` instead of `.transfer` intentionally here. Using `.transfer` would allow any user to lock up our contract by investing from a poorly written or malicious contract. By using `.send`, an investor who sends ether from a poorly written or malicious contract will simply never receive any ether. In such a scenario, `.send` will fail and return false, we will ignore the return value, and the contract will overwrite their address with the new investor. The ether will remain in the contract and be unclaimable. Note that `.send` forwards only 2,300 gas when sending to a contract, so we will be safe from re-entrancy attacks as well.

This is a common theme you will be observing in the contracts we write. Whenever possible, we will deter attackers by imposing a monetary penalty for attempting a hack. If in the process a few well-intentioned developers get penalized for their errors, that is a collateral we are willing to accept. In blockchain engineering, security is paramount. All else is a secondary consideration.

As always, deploying this contract requires a migration. Listing 7-5 presents the migration without explanation. For an explanation, see Chapter 3.

Listing 7-5. Simple Ponzi Migration

```
var fs = require('fs');
var SimplePonzi = artifacts.require("SimplePonzi");

module.exports = function(deployer, network) {
```

```
    // unlock account for geth
    if (network == "rinkeby" || network == "mainnet") {
        var password = fs.readFileSync("password", "utf8")
                        .split('\n')[0];
        web3.personal.unlockAccount(
            web3.eth.accounts[0], password);
    }

    deployer.deploy(SimplePonzi);
};
```

A copy of this migration can be found on our GitHub repo at
https://github.com/k26dr/ethereum-games/blob/master/
migrations/6_simple_ponzi.js. Run the code in Listing 7-6 to deploy
the contract to a private net. The first line opens the Truffle development
environment, and the second deploys the contract. We assume that your
migration has the same number as ours. If it doesn't, replace 6 with the
appropriate number.

Listing 7-6. Deploy Simple Ponzi

```
truffle develop
migrate -f 6
```

We're going to run through a sample interaction with the contract in
Listing 7-7. We will invest in the contract with two separate accounts and
watch the money flow from the second investor to the first.

Listing 7-7. Interacting with the Simple Ponzi

```
// The following lines should be entered one by one into
// the same truffle dev environment as Listing 6-7

accounts = web3.eth.accounts
```

```
web3.eth.sendTransaction({ from: accounts[0], to: SimplePonzi.
address, value: 1e18 })

web3.eth.getBalance(accounts[0]) // first check

web3.eth.sendTransaction({ from: accounts[1], to: SimplePonzi.
address, value: 1e17 }) // error

web3.eth.sendTransaction({ from: accounts[1], to: SimplePonzi.
address, value: 2e18 })

web3.eth.getBalance(accounts[0]) // second check
```

The first attempt to invest by accounts[1] sends less ether than the investment by accounts[0], so it will be rejected. Between the first and second balance checks, you should see the balance of the account increase by 2 ether, which is the amount sent by the second address. Let's make this a little more real in Exercises 7-1 and 7-2 by running the same code on the mainnet.

EXERCISE 7-1. INVESTMENT OF A LIFETIME!

Ponzis aren't fun if nobody's making or losing money, so we've deployed our SimplePonzi contract to the Ethereum mainnet to allow readers to get in on the fun. You can view the contract source, view the current investment, and see a history of transactions at https://etherscan.io/address/0xd09180f 956c97a165c23c7f932908600c2e3e0fb. This contract is a real live Ponzi. You will get a return on your investment only if someone invests after you. We have seeded the contract with 0.005 ether to get the Ponzi started. May the brave be rewarded with riches.

EXERCISE 7-2. MY FIRST HACK

A minor security flaw in the SimplePonzi contract can render it nearly unusable. Describing it further would make it too easy to find, so we won't. Can you find it and exploit it? A 0.1 ether reward will be given to the first user to reply with a link to a transaction that exploits the flaw on the GitHub issue (`https://github.com/k26dr/ethereum-games/issues/1`). Alternatively, any user who manages to steal ether from the contract or another user will also receive the reward, but don't expect such a flaw to exist!

Realistic Ponzi

Our SimplePonzi was simple to create and created a suspenseful scenario in which users aren't sure whether they will receive their money back. Real Ponzis, however, tend to pay out investors gradually with above-average percentage returns until the Ponzi gets too large to sustain. Let's write a contract (Listing 7-8) that captures this more realistic scenario. Again, we will go through this in blocks to explain things more clearly, so don't worry if you don't grasp all of it at once.

Listing 7-8. A More Realistic Gradual Ponzi

```
contract GradualPonzi {
    address[] public investors;
    mapping (address => uint) public balances;
    uint public constant MINIMUM_INVESTMENT = 1e15;

    function GradualPonzi () public {
        investors.push(msg.sender);
    }
```

```
function () public payable {
    require(msg.value >= MINIMUM_INVESTMENT);
    uint eachInvestorGets = msg.value /
                            investors.length;
    for (uint i=0; i < investors.length; i++) {
        balances[investors[i]] += eachInvestorGets;
    }
    investors.push(msg.sender);
}

function withdraw () public {
    uint payout = balances[msg.sender];
    balances[msg.sender] = 0;
    msg.sender.transfer(payout);
}
}
```

This gradual Ponzi has three state variables and three functions. Because we have a significantly greater number of payouts to handle, we will use a withdrawal function and internal balances instead of sending ether directly. Additionally, we have added a minimum investment to prevent freeloaders from sending a 0-value transaction to become an investor. Because new investments are distributed evenly between investors, there is no incentive to send more than the minimum payment. This was done to avoid adding the complexity of tracking investor shares.

Let's walk through the code in blocks, starting with the variables and constructor in Listing 7-9.

Listing 7-9. GradualPonzi Variables and Constructor

```
contract GradualPonzi {
    address[] public investors;
    mapping (address => uint) public balances;
    uint public constant MINIMUM_INVESTMENT = 1e15;

    function GradualPonzi () public {
        investors.push(msg.sender);
    }
```

This sets up two state variables and a minimum investment constant. The constructor adds the contract creator as the first investor. Because there's no one else available to send money to, the creator gets the privilege of joining the Ponzi without having to send any ether.

Investors must meet the minimum investment to join the Ponzi. When they send in their ether, their investment is distributed evenly among all investors (Listing 7-10).

Listing 7-10. GradualPonzi Investment Logic

```
function () public payable {
    require(msg.value >= MINIMUM_INVESTMENT);
    uint eachInvestorGets = msg.value / investors.length;
    for (uint i=0; i < investors.length; i++) {
        balances[investors[i]] += eachInvestorGets;
    }
    investors.push(msg.sender);
}
```

As the number of investors in the Ponzi increases, the return for an investor from each new investment decreases. After the distribution is complete, the newest investor is added to the list of investors (Listing 7-11).

Listing 7-11. GradualPonzi Withdrawals

```
function withdraw () public {
    uint payout = balances[msg.sender];
    balances[msg.sender] = 0;
    msg.sender.transfer(payout);
}
```

The migration for this contract can be found on the GitHub repo at `https://github.com/k26dr/ethereum-games/blob/master/migrations/7_gradual_ponzi.js`. It is a standard migration, so it is offered without explanation in Listing 7-12.

Listing 7-12. GradualPonzi Migration

```
var fs = require('fs');
var GradualPonzi = artifacts.require("GradualPonzi");

module.exports = function(deployer, network) {

    // unlock account for geth
    if (network == "rinkeby" || network == "mainnet") {
        var password = fs.readFileSync("password", "utf8")
                          .split('\n')[0];
        web3.personal.unlockAccount(web3.eth.accounts[0], password);
    }

    deployer.deploy(GradualPonzi);
};
```

Open a Truffle dev console with `truffle develop`. We're going to deploy and then interact with the contract in the dev console. Enter the code in Listing 7-13 into the dev console one line at a time.

Listing 7-13. Deploying and Using GradualPonzi

```
migrate -f 7

ponzi = GradualPonzi.at(GradualPonzi.address)

web3.eth.sendTransaction({ from: web3.eth.accounts[1], to:
ponzi.address, value: 1e15, gas: 200e3 })

ponzi.balances(web3.eth.accounts[0])

ponzi.withdraw({ from: web3.eth.accounts[0] })
```

The first line deploys the contract. If you used a different number than us for your migration, change the 7 to your migration number. The rest of the lines run through a sample interaction with the contract. Account 1 invests in the Ponzi by sending 0.001 ether to the contract, and then Account 0 checks his balance and withdraws. Because Account 0 is the only existing investor when Account 1 invests, all the ether goes to Account 0. In subsequent investments, the money will be split between multiple investors. You will be running a more in-depth interaction with the contract in Exercise 7-3 before having a chance to invest real ether on the mainnet in Exercise 7-4.

EXERCISE 7-3. GRADUAL PONZI

Use the sample code from Listing 7-13 to run a series of 10 investments, one from each of the accounts in the Truffle dev console. After running all the investments, check the balances of each of the accounts. The distribution of returns should follow a classic Ponzi, with the earliest investor receiving the most, and the latest investor receiving the least.

EXERCISE 7-4. THE BEAUTIFUL PONZI

We have deployed a version of the GradualPonzi contract to the mainnet. The transaction history and contract state can be read at `https://etherscan.io/address/0xf89e29fd10716757d1d3d2997975c639c8750e92`. Get in on the Ponzi by sending .001 ether to the contract. Get in early enough, and you'll get a handsome return. How early is early enough? You'll have to play to find out.

Simple Pyramid

Pyramids are a little more complex than Ponzis because they require the creation of an ever-widening pyramid and staggered payouts to participants. We've constructed a SimplePyramid contract in Listing 7-14 that works in layers. Each layer is twice as large as the previous layer. Each layer receives its investment back when the next layer fills. The leftover ether is then distributed among all participants.

Listing 7-14. SimplePyramid

```
contract SimplePyramid {

    uint public constant MINIMUM_INVESTMENT = 1e15; // 0.001 ether
    uint public numInvestors = 0;
    uint public depth = 0;
    address[] public investors;
    mapping(address => uint) public balances;

    function SimplePyramid () public payable {
        require(msg.value >= MINIMUM_INVESTMENT);
        investors.length = 3;
        investors[0] = msg.sender;
```

```
        numInvestors = 1;
        depth = 1;
        balances[address(this)] = msg.value;
    }

    function () payable public {
        require(msg.value >= MINIMUM_INVESTMENT);
        balances[address(this)] += msg.value;

        numInvestors += 1;
        investors[numInvestors - 1] = msg.sender;

        if (numInvestors == investors.length) {
            // pay out previous layer
            uint endIndex = numInvestors - 2**depth;
            uint startIndex = endIndex - 2**(depth-1);
            for (uint i = startIndex; i < endIndex; i++)
                balances[investors[i]] += MINIMUM_INVESTMENT;

            // spread remaining ether among all participants
            uint paid = MINIMUM_INVESTMENT * 2**(depth-1);
            uint eachInvestorGets = (balances[address(this)]
            - paid) /
                                    numInvestors;
            for(i = 0; i < numInvestors; i++)
                balances[investors[i]] += eachInvestorGets;

            // update state variables
            balances[address(this)] = 0;
            depth += 1;
            investors.length += 2**depth;
        }
    }
```

```
function withdraw () public {
    uint payout = balances[msg.sender];
    balances[msg.sender] = 0;
    msg.sender.transfer(payout);
}
}
```

Let's go through this and break it down into easier-to-understand blocks starting with the variables in Listing 7-15.

Listing 7-15. SimplePyramid Variables

```
contract SimplePyramid {
    uint public constant MINIMUM_INVESTMENT = 1e15;
    uint public numInvestors = 0;
    uint public depth = 0;
    address[] public investors;
    mapping(address => uint) public balances;
```

The opening block of code declares four variables and a constant. All the variables and constants are public:

- MINIMUM_INVESTMENT: The minimum amount required to participate in the contract. Sending more than the minimum has no benefit and is not advised. We've set it to 1^{15} wei, or 0.001 ether, to make it easy to participate, but you can modify this up to create a high-stakes pyramid.

- numInvestors: A running internal count of the number of addresses that have invested so far.

157

- depth: The current pyramid level. The number of investors in a level is 2^{depth}. Payouts occur as each subsequent layer fills. Because the layer sizes are increasing exponentially, they will eventually get too large to fill. The first layer is depth = 0 and contains one investor, the second layer (depth = 1) contains two investors, the third layer (depth = 2) contains four investors, and so forth.

- investors: An array containing every address that has invested so far, in order. Because the investors are in order, the level at which the investment occurred can be calculated from the investor's position in the array.

- balances: A standard internal ledger of ether balances.

Listing 7-16 displays the constructor logic.

Listing 7-16. SimplyPyramid Constructor

```
function SimplePyramid () public payable {
    require(msg.value >= MINIMUM_INVESTMENT);
    investors.length = 3;
    investors[0] = msg.sender;
    numInvestors = 1;
    depth = 1;
    balances[address(this)] = msg.value;
}
```

The constructor requires the creator of the contract to become the first investor. The creator must send at least the minimum investment. Initially, open slots are available for three investors. The creator of the contract is by himself in the first layer, and the second layer has two unfilled slots. No payouts are made until the second layer fills, so the initial investment is added to the contract's internal balance.

Listing 7-17 contains the initial portion of the investment logic.

Listing 7-17. SimplePyramid Investment Logic

```
function () payable public {
    require(msg.value >= MINIMUM_INVESTMENT);
    balances[address(this)] += msg.value;

    numInvestors += 1;
    investors[numInvestors - 1] = msg.sender;
```

For a basic investment that doesn't fill a layer and trigger a payout, the contract updates only state variables. If the investment exceeds the minimum investment, the contract's internal balance is updated with the investment value, and the investor is added to the end of the investors array.

If the latest investor fills a layer in the pyramid, the payout logic in Listing 7-18 executes.

Listing 7-18. SimplePyramid Repayments

```
if (numInvestors == investors.length) {
    // pay out previous layer
    uint endIndex = numInvestors - 2**depth;
    uint startIndex = endIndex - 2**(depth-1);
    for (uint i = startIndex; i < endIndex; i++)
        balances[investors[i]] += MINIMUM_INVESTMENT;
```

We start by paying back the previous layer their initial investment. Because each layer contains 2^{depth} participants, the end of the previous layer can be determined by going back 2^{depth} indexes in the array. That previous layer is only half as large as the current layer, so the start of that layer will be the $2^{depth-1}$ indexes back from the end of the layer. Looping from the start to the end index of the layer, the internal balances of each investor are paid back their initial investment.

Once the previous layer has been repaid, the remaining ether in the contract is distributed evenly among all members (Listing 7-19).

Listing 7-19. SimplePyramid Interest Payments

```
// spread remaining ether among all participants
uint paid = MINIMUM_INVESTMENT * 2**(depth-1);
uint eachInvestorGets = (balances[address(this)] - paid) /
                        numInvestors;
for(i = 0; i < numInvestors; i++)
    balances[investors[i]] += eachInvestorGets;
```

To determine the amount paid out as repayments, the minimum investment is multiplied by the size of the previous layer, $2^{depth-1}$. The remainder is split evenly and added to the internal balances of each investor (Listing 7-20).

Listing 7-20. SimplePyramid Adding a Layer

```
// update state variables
balances[address(this)] = 0;
depth += 1;
investors.length += 2**depth;
```

The contract's internal balance is zeroed because it has been distributed among the investors, the depth increases, and the investors array is lengthened to accommodate the next layer of investors.

The contract uses a standard withdrawal function (Listing 7-21). See Chapter 4 for an explanation.

Listing 7-21. SimplePyramid Withdrawals

```
function withdraw () public {
    uint payout = balances[msg.sender];
```

```
    balances[msg.sender] = 0;
    msg.sender.transfer(payout);
}
```

The migration for this contract is standard with one exception: a value of 1^{15} wei is included with the deployment for the initial investment. The full migration can be found on the GitHub repo at `https://github.com/k26dr/ethereum-games/blob/master/migrations/8_simple_pyramid.js`. Only the nonstandard line is printed here:

```
deployer.deploy(SimplePyramid, { value: 1e15 });
```

To deploy the contract to a private network, use Listing 7-22 in the Truffle dev console. As always, replace our migration number (8) with your custom migration number if necessary.

Listing 7-22. Deploying SimplePyramid

```
truffle develop

# The following commands go in the opened dev console
migrate -f 8
pyramid = SimplePyramid.at(SimplePyramid.address)
```

This creates a pointer variable to the deployed contract. We will be using that pointer to interact with the contract in Exercise 7-5.

EXERCISE 7-5. PYRAMID DISTRIBUTIONS

In the Truffle dev console, use the `pyramid` variable created in Listing 7-22 to interact with your SimplePyramid. Use the 10 accounts created by Truffle to fill up the first three layers and then watch the investments get redistributed among the pyramid.

When you feel comfortable using the pyramid scheme on a private network, Exercise 7-6 will allow you to join the scheme on the mainnet.

EXERCISE 7-6. ROAD TO DESTITUTION

We have deployed a version of our SimplePyramid to the mainnet so that you can be scammed too. The minimum investment is set to a reasonable 0.001 ether so that you don't have to worry about losing too much money to play. If you get in early, you might even make money. Use the geth console to send .001 ether to the pyramid scheme and track the activity on Etherscan. The contract code and state can be read at `https://etherscan.io/address/0x9b0033bccf2d913dd17c08a5844c9dd31dd34833`.

Governmental

Governmental was a complex pyramid scheme that ran on the Ethereum mainnet for about 40 days in early 2016. It was one of the most popular contracts on the Ethereum network at the time. The rules and code for the game are reproduced in Listings 7-23 and 7-24, respectively. You can also see the rules at `http://governmental.github.io/GovernMental/` and the code at `https://etherscan.io/address/0xf45717552f12ef7cb65e95476 f217ea008167ae3#code`.

Listing 7-23. Governmental Rules

- You can lend the government money; they promise to pay it back with 10% interest. Minimum contribution is 1 ether.

- If the government does not receive new money for 12 hours, the system breaks down. The latest creditor saw the crash coming and receives the jackpot. All others will lose their claims.

- All incoming money is used in the following way: 5% goes into the "jackpot" (capped at 10,000 ether); 5% goes to the corrupt elite that runs the government; 90% is used to pay out creditors in order of their date of credit. When the jackpot is full, 95% goes toward the payout of creditors.

- Creditors can share an affiliate link. Money deposited this way is distributed as follows: 5% goes toward the linker directly, 5% to the corrupt elite, 5% into the jackpot (until full). The rest is used for payouts.

Listing 7-24. Governmental Code

```
contract Government {

    // Global Variables
    uint32 public lastCreditorPayedOut;
    uint public lastTimeOfNewCredit;
    uint public profitFromCrash;
    address[] public creditorAddresses;
    uint[] public creditorAmounts;
    address public corruptElite;
    mapping (address => uint) buddies;
    uint constant TWELVE_HOURS = 43200;
    uint8 public round;

    function Government() {
        // The corrupt elite establishes a new government
        // this is the commitment of the corrupt Elite -
        // everything that can not be saved from a crash
        profitFromCrash = msg.value;
        corruptElite = msg.sender;
```

```
        lastTimeOfNewCredit = block.timestamp;
    }

    function lendGovernmentMoney(address buddy) returns (bool) {
        uint amount = msg.value;
        // check if the system already broke down. If for 12h no
        // new creditor gives new credit to the system it will
        brake down.
        // 12h are on average = 60*60*12/12.5 = 3456
        if (lastTimeOfNewCredit + TWELVE_HOURS < block.timestamp) {
            // Return money to sender
            msg.sender.send(amount);
            // Sends all contract money to the last creditor
            creditorAddresses[creditorAddresses.length - 1]
                .send(profitFromCrash);
            corruptElite.send(this.balance);
            // Reset contract state
            lastCreditorPayedOut = 0;
            lastTimeOfNewCredit = block.timestamp;
            profitFromCrash = 0;
            creditorAddresses = new address[](0);
            creditorAmounts = new uint[](0);
            round += 1;
            return false;
        }
        else {
            // the system needs to collect at least 1% of the profit
            // from a crash to stay alive
            if (amount >= 10 ** 18) {
                // the System has received fresh money,
                // it will survive at least 12h more
                lastTimeOfNewCredit = block.timestamp;
```

```
// register the new creditor and his amount with
// 10% interest rate
creditorAddresses.push(msg.sender);
creditorAmounts.push(amount * 110 / 100);
// now the money is distributed
// first the corrupt elite grabs 5% - thieves!
corruptElite.send(amount * 5/100);
// 5% are going into the economy (they will
increase
// the value for the person seeing the crash coming)
if (profitFromCrash < 10000 * 10**18) {
    profitFromCrash += amount * 5/100;
}
// if you have a buddy in the government (and he is
// in the creditor list) he can get 5% of your
credits.
// Make a deal with him.
if(buddies[buddy] >= amount) {
    buddy.send(amount * 5/100);
}
buddies[msg.sender] += amount * 110 / 100;
// 90% of the money will be used to pay out old
creditors
if (creditorAmounts[lastCreditorPayedOut] <=
    address(this).balance - profitFromCrash) {
    creditorAddresses[lastCreditorPayedOut].send(
        creditorAmounts[lastCreditorPayedOut]);
    buddies[creditorAddresses[lastCreditorPayed
    Out]] -=
        creditorAmounts[lastCreditorPayedOut];
    lastCreditorPayedOut += 1;
```

```
                }
            return true;
        }
        else {
            msg.sender.send(amount);
            return false;
        }
    }
}

// fallback function
function() {
    lendGovernmentMoney(0);
}

function totalDebt() returns (uint debt) {
    for(uint i=lastCreditorPayedOut; i<creditorAmounts.
    length; i++){
        debt += creditorAmounts[i];
    }
}

function totalPayedOut() returns (uint payout) {
    for(uint i=0; i<lastCreditorPayedOut; i++){
        payout += creditorAmounts[i];
    }
}

// better don't do it
// (unless you are the corrupt elite and you
// want to establish trust in the system)
function investInTheSystem() {
    profitFromCrash += msg.value;
}
```

```
// From time to time the corrupt elite inherits
// it's power to the next generation
function inheritToNextGeneration(address nextGeneration) {
    if (msg.sender == corruptElite) {
        corruptElite = nextGeneration;
    }
}

function getCreditorAddresses() returns (address[]) {
    return creditorAddresses;
}

function getCreditorAmounts() returns (uint[]) {
    return creditorAmounts;
}
}
```

As a warning, this code will not work properly on the latest version of Solidity. It uses a few quirks of the language that have been deprecated since the contract was written. A version of the code that works with the most recent version of Solidity is available on the GitHub repo at `contracts/Governmental.sol`. You can deploy and interact with that one if you wish. Doing so will be left as an exercise for you.

The code is well commented, so we won't go through the entirety of it in detail as we did with the other contracts. We will cover only the portions that are difficult to understand, starting with the variables in Listing 7-25.

Listing 7-25. Governmental Variables

```
// Global Variables
uint32 public lastCreditorPayedOut;
uint public lastTimeOfNewCredit;
uint public profitFromCrash;
```

```
address[] public creditorAddresses;
uint[] public creditorAmounts;
address public corruptElite;
mapping (address => uint) buddies;
uint constant TWELVE_HOURS = 43200;
uint8 public round;
```

Understanding the state variables in use will get us halfway to understanding the contract itself. Let's go through them:

- lastCreditorPayedOut: This is a poorly named variable. It stores the index of the first creditor that hasn't been paid out. It is used in conjunction with creditorAddresses and creditorAmounts.

- lastTimeOfNewCredit: This is a UNIX timestamp storing the timestamp of the last investment. If a new investment doesn't arrive within 12 hours, the Ponzi "collapses," and the last creditor receives the jackpot.

- profitFromCrash: This is the jackpot that the last creditor stands to win. It is seeded within an initial amount from the corrupt elite and added to by 5% of every creditor's investment.

- creditorAddresses: A list of creditor addresses. cred itorAddresses[lastCreditorPayedOut] refers to the first creditor in line that hasn't been paid out.

- creditorAmounts: A list of the amounts owed to each creditor. creditorAmounts[lastCreditorPayedOut] refers to the amount owed to the first creditor in line that hasn't been paid out.

- corruptElite: The creator of the contract. This address receives 5% of every investment.

- buddies: A mapping of creditor addresses to creditor amounts. It's a redundant combination of creditorAddresses and creditorAmounts, but it's much faster for lookup of a single address because it's a mapping instead of an array. Used to determine affiliate bonuses.

- TWELVE_HOURS: A constant—12 hours in seconds.

- round: Every time a jackpot is paid out, a new round begins. In theory, the game could go on forever. In practice, see what happened when the game got too large in Chapter 5.

If you understand the variables, the payout of creditors is the only other portion of the contract that is difficult to interpret (Listing 7-26).

Listing 7-26. Governmental Creditor Payouts

```
// 90% of the money will be used to pay out old creditors
if (creditorAmounts[lastCreditorPayedOut] <=
    address(this).balance - profitFromCrash) {

    creditorAddresses[lastCreditorPayedOut].send(
        creditorAmounts[lastCreditorPayedOut]);

    buddies[creditorAddresses[lastCreditorPayedOut]] -=
        creditorAmounts[lastCreditorPayedOut];

    lastCreditorPayedOut += 1;
}
```

We've added spacing between each line to make the code more readable. The if condition resolves only if paying out the next creditor will leave enough ether in the contract to pay out a jackpot. The jackpot is given priority over creditor repayments. This means that a stack of unpaid creditors can potentially line up.

If there is enough ether in the contract to pay out the next creditor, the amount owed to that creditor is sent to the creditor's address. Remember, the amount owed to the creditor includes a 10% markup on their initial investment.

The third line here subtracts the amount paid out from the buddies list. This line could be simplified by setting the value to zero. After an address has been paid out, they can no longer claim referral bonuses. The final line then increments the creditor index so the next creditor can be paid in the next transaction.

Summary

This chapter went through a series of pyramid and Ponzi contracts and exposed you to your first real-world contract, Governmental. Mainnet deployments for SimplePonzi, GradualPonzi, and SimplePyramid are all available for you to use in collaboration with other readers. Ponzis and pyramids formed the first exploration of some of the unique game designs Ethereum makes possible. We will continue this exploration in the next chapter with lotteries.

CHAPTER 8

Lotteries

Lotteries are an excellent use case for Ethereum. Like pyramids, lotteries were among the first contracts on the Ethereum blockchain. Results are provably fair, enabling the lottery to be run without a central authority taking a cut of the winnings, and without anchoring its operation in any single legal jurisdiction. It is highly likely that the lotteries of the future will be conducted on a blockchain. This chapter covers the primary roadblock to running a good lottery—random-number generation—and develops a series of increasingly complex lottery contracts.

Note   All the code for this chapter is available in our GitHub repo at https://github.com/k26dr/ethereum-games/blob/master/contracts/Lotteries.sol.

Random-Number Generation

We covered random-number generation (RNG) in detail in Chapter 5. As a brief overview, our primary options for a source of entropy are the blockhash and external oracles. To minimize complexity and external dependencies, we will be using blockhashes for our random numbers.

  Because only the previous blockhash is available to us, and it is known at the time the transaction is executed, we will have to take additional measures to make the final result unpredictable. Specifically, we will be

© Kedar Iyer and Chris Dannen 2018
K. Iyer and C. Dannen, *Building Games with Ethereum Smart Contracts*,
https://doi.org/10.1007/978-1-4842-3492-1_8

instituting time delays between the ticket purchase period and the drawing of the winner, so that the blockhash used to determine the winner is not known at any point when lottery tickets are being distributed.

We mentioned in Chapter 5 that we can create a better RNG by using lotteries. We will be doing that later in this chapter. It is more complex and less user-friendly than using the blockhash, but in return it provides a better source of entropy.

Simple Lottery

We will start with the simplest lottery possible. Our simple lottery will be nonrecurring, uses blockhashes for random numbers, and has only one winner. We present the code in its entirety first (Listing 8-1) before explaining in detail.

Listing 8-1. A Simple Lottery

```
contract SimpleLottery {
    uint public constant TICKET_PRICE = 1e16; // 0.01 ether

    address[] public tickets;
    address public winner;
    uint public ticketingCloses;

    function SimpleLottery (uint duration) public {
        ticketingCloses = now + duration;
    }

    function buy () public payable {
        require(msg.value == TICKET_PRICE);
        require(now < ticketingCloses);

        tickets.push(msg.sender);
    }
```

```
function drawWinner () public {
    require(now > ticketingCloses + 5 minutes);
    require(winner == address(0));

    bytes32 rand = keccak256(
        block.blockhash(block.number-1)
    );
    winner = tickets[uint(rand) % tickets.length];
}

function withdraw () public {
    require(msg.sender == winner);
    msg.sender.transfer(this.balance);
}

function () payable public {
    buy();
}
}
```

The lottery has a constructor and three public functions corresponding to the three actions a user can take: buy a ticket, draw a winner, and claim their winnings. By default, the fallback function buys a ticket if a user sends ether to the contract address.

Reviewing the state variables and constants declared in the contract will give us a good feel for the implementation details:

- TICKET_PRICE: The price of a lottery ticket. When a user buys a ticket, they will be sending this value along with their transaction.

- tickets: A list of addresses that have bought tickets. An address can be in the array multiple times if the user buys multiple tickets.

- `winner`: The winner of the lottery. This is the user who gets to claim the prize. The prize cannot be withdrawn until the winner is set.

- `ticketingCloses`: A UNIX timestamp. Tickets can be purchased up until this time. The winner is drawn at least 5 minutes after this time so that the random blockhash is unknown during the ticketing process.

The only variable that needs to be set at contract creation is `ticketingCloses`. The duration of the contract is specified as the argument to the constructor, and the ticket close time is set to `duration` seconds in the future.

Because the constructor takes an argument, that argument needs to be passed in from the migration. The full migration is available in the GitHub repo at `https://github.com/k26dr/ethereum-games/blob/master/migrations/9_simple_lottery.js`. Listing 8-2 lists only the nonstandard portions of the migration in which the constructor argument is specified.

Listing 8-2. SimpleLottery Migration with Constructor Arguments

```
...
    var duration = 3600 * 24 * 3; // 3 days
    deployer.deploy(SimpleLottery, duration);
};
```

Buying a ticket is fairly simple, so we will cover it briefly without reprinting. The value must be exactly equal to the ticket price, and the transaction must be mined before the ticketing close time. Buying a ticket adds the sender's address to the tickets array.

Drawing a winner (Listing 8-3) picks a random address from the tickets array.

Listing 8-3. Drawing a Winner in SimpleLottery

```
function drawWinner () public {
    require(now > ticketingCloses + 5 minutes);
    require(winner == address(0));
    bytes32 rand = keccak256(
        block.blockhash(block.number-1)
    );
    winner = tickets[uint(rand) % tickets.length];
}
```

Picking a winner requires the ticketing window to be closed for at least 5 minutes. This is done to ensure no one can know the blockhash, our source of entropy, while buying a ticket. Checking that the winning address is currently set to the zero address ensures that the winner hasn't already been picked.

We generate a random sequence of bytes by hashing the most recent blockhash. Converting those bytes into an integer and then using the modulus to bound the range of the number yields a random index. The winning address is the address located at the randomly generated index in the tickets array.

We have seen the remaining two functions in the contract before. The withdrawal function is standard and sends the whole contract balance to the winner. The fallback function simply executes a buy. In Exercise 8-1, modify the lottery code so that we can quickly run an end-to-end interaction with the contract.

EXERCISE 8-1. QUICK LOTTERY

Change the wait period before drawing a winner from 5 minutes to 1 minute
and set the duration of the lottery to 1 minute in the migration. Deploy the
modified lottery to a private chain and use a loop to purchase a ticket for each
of the 10 accounts. Wait a couple of minutes for the ticketing and waiting
periods to end, and then draw a winner and claim the prize from the winning
address. All contract variables are public, so you should be able to track the
state of the contract as you go.

Recurring Lottery

The lottery we wrote in the previous section focused on simplicity while
sacrificing real-world usability. In this section, we're going to build a
more realistic lottery contract that can be deployed to the mainnet. The
new lottery will occur in rounds so that a new prize pool is started every
time the old one closes. It will also allow users to purchase multiple
tickets in one transaction instead of just one and add a couple of security
improvements. Listing 8-4 displays the whole contract before we get into
the details of the code.

Listing 8-4. Recurring, Multiticket Lottery

```
contract RecurringLottery {
    struct Round {
        uint endBlock;
        uint drawBlock;
        Entry[] entries;
        uint totalQuantity;
        address winner;
    }
```

```
struct Entry {
    address buyer;
    uint quantity;
}

uint constant public TICKET_PRICE = 1e15;

mapping(uint => Round) public rounds;
uint public round;
uint public duration;
mapping (address => uint) public balances;

// duration is in blocks. 1 day = ~5500 blocks
function RecurringLottery (uint _duration) public {
    duration = _duration;
    round = 1;
    rounds[round].endBlock = block.number + duration;
    rounds[round].drawBlock = block.number + duration + 5;
}

function buy () payable public {
    require(msg.value % TICKET_PRICE == 0);

    if (block.number > rounds[round].endBlock) {
        round += 1;
        rounds[round].endBlock = block.number + duration;
        rounds[round].drawBlock = block.number + duration + 5;
    }

    uint quantity = msg.value / TICKET_PRICE;
    Entry memory entry = Entry(msg.sender, quantity);
    rounds[round].entries.push(entry);
    rounds[round].totalQuantity += quantity;
}
```

```solidity
function drawWinner (uint roundNumber) public {
    Round storage drawing = rounds[roundNumber];
    require(drawing.winner ==  address(0));
    require(block.number > drawing.drawBlock);
    require(drawing.entries.length > 0);

    // pick winner
    bytes32 rand = keccak256(
        block.blockhash(drawing.drawBlock)
    );
    uint counter = uint(rand) % drawing.totalQuantity;
    for (uint i=0; i < drawing.entries.length; i++) {
        uint quantity = drawing.entries[i].quantity;
        if (quantity > counter) {
            drawing.winner = drawing.entries[i].buyer;
            break;
        }
        else
            counter -= quantity;
    }

    balances[drawing.winner] += TICKET_PRICE * drawing.
    totalQuantity;
}

function withdraw () public {
    uint amount = balances[msg.sender];
    balances[msg.sender] = 0;
    msg.sender.transfer(amount);
}
```

```
function deleteRound (uint _round) public {
    require(block.number > rounds[_round].drawBlock + 100);
    require(rounds[_round].winner != address(0));
    delete rounds[_round];
}

function () payable public {
    buy();
}
}
```

As you can see, this is a much more complex contract than our simple lottery. Some functionality is reused, but for the most part it is a brand- new contract.

Constants and Variables

We have a couple of structs defined at the top of our contract before the state variables (Listing 8-5).

Listing 8-5. RecurringLottery Struct Definitions

```
struct Round {
    uint endBlock;
    uint drawBlock;
    Entry[] entries;
    uint totalQuantity;
    address winner;
}
struct Entry {
    address buyer;
    uint quantity;
}
```

179

Type and struct definitions usually go at the beginning of a contract because they are used in the variable definitions and rest of the contract. We have defined two structs: Round and Entry.

A round ends when block number endBlock is mined and the winner is determined by selecting a random entry from entries. A random seed generated by the blockhash from block number drawBlock will determine which entry gets the prize. A single Entry contains the buyer address and quantity of tickets purchased. Since an Entry can hold more than one ticket, determining the total number of tickets sold requires a calculation that gets more expensive with more entries. Instead, totalQuantity is defined to track the number of tickets sold in each round.

The majority of the state complexity is captured in the struct definitions, so the state variables and constants in the contract are minimal:

- TICKET_PRICE: The price of a single ticket. This can be small because multiple tickets can be purchased at once.

- round: The round number. This variable allows the lottery to be recurring.

- rounds: A mapping from round numbers to Round structs.

- duration: The duration of a single round in blocks. One day spans approximately 5,500 blocks.

- balances: A standard mapping of user balances.

The constructor function (Listing 8-6) has to initialize a few variables this time.

Listing 8-6. RecurringLottery Constructor

```
function RecurringLottery (uint _duration) public {
    duration = _duration;
    round = 1;
    rounds[round].endBlock = block.number + duration;
    rounds[round].drawBlock = block.number + duration + 5;
}
```

The duration and times are measured in blocks instead of seconds this time. This is because we care about the number of blocks between ticketing and drawing, not the number of seconds since block times can be varied. The `endBlock` and `drawBlock` are set five blocks apart so that the blockhash is unknown to all participants.

Gameplay

The round incrementing logic is handled during the ticket purchase (Listing 8-7).

Listing 8-7. Round Incrementing Logic

```
function buy () payable public {
    require(msg.value % TICKET_PRICE == 0);

    if (block.number > rounds[round].endBlock) {
        round += 1;
        rounds[round].endBlock = block.number + duration;
        rounds[round].drawBlock = block.number +
            duration + 5;
    }
    ...
```

First, we check to make sure the ether value of the transaction is a multiple of the ticket price. Multiple tickets can be purchased at once, but fractional tickets are not allowed. Then we check to see whether the current round has expired. If it has, we increment the round counter and set end and draw times for the new round. The ticket purchase will still go through, but it will be the first purchase of the new round.

Listing 8-8 details the ticket purchase logic in the second half of the buy function.

Listing 8-8. Ticket Purchase Logic

```
...
uint quantity = msg.value / TICKET_PRICE;
Entry memory entry = Entry(msg.sender, quantity);
rounds[round].entries.push(entry);
rounds[round].totalQuantity += quantity;
}
```

The quantity of tickets purchased is the multiple of the ticket price sent with the transaction. This is a payable function so it can receive ether.

The second line is interesting. It's the first time we've explicitly used the memory modifier in one of our contracts. Solidity automatically creates constructors for all structs. These constructors take the properties of the struct in order as arguments. When the struct is created, it is created in memory, not storage. If you omit the memory modifier, Solidity will create a storage Entry pointer by default. The compiler will throw a type mismatch error because the value of type memory Entry cannot be referenced by a storage Entry pointer (Figure 8-1).

```
,/home/kedar/code/ethereum-games/contracts/Lotteries.sol:82:9: TypeError: Type struct R
ecurringLottery.Entry memory is not implicitly convertible to expected type struct Recu
rringLottery.Entry storage pointer.
        Entry entry = Entry(msg.sender, quantity);
        ^-----------------------------------------^
```

Figure 8-1. *Type mismatch error between storage and memory*

When a memory struct is pushed to a storage array, Solidity automatically converts the memory struct to a storage struct before pushing the item to the array. This is why the third line in Listing 8-8 does not throw an error.

After a round has ended, there is a five-block waiting period before a winner can be drawn. Five blocks is far enough out in the future that no one can know the blockhash ahead of time. Minimally, two would be enough because the latest available blockhash is from the previous block (see "Random-Number Generation" in Chapter 5 for an explanation), but we will wait five to be safe.

Listing 8-9 reproduces the first half of the drawWinner function. The function takes a round number as an argument.

Listing 8-9. Initial Conditions and Local Variables for Drawing a Winner

```
function drawWinner (uint roundNumber) public {
    Round storage drawing = rounds[roundNumber];
    require(drawing.winner == address(0));
    require(block.number > drawing.drawBlock);
    require(drawing.entries.length > 0);

    // pick winner
    bytes32 rand = keccak256(
        block.blockhash(drawing.drawBlock)
    );
    uint counter = uint(rand) % drawing.totalQuantity;
    ...
```

Three checks are performed. The first ensures that a winner hasn't already been set for the specified round, the second verifies that the `drawBlock` blockhash is now available, and the third ensures that at least one ticket was purchased. Anybody can trigger the `drawWinner` function for any round at any time, but these checks combine to ensure that it will run successfully only once.

Regardless of when the drawing occurs, the random-number generator uses the blockhash specifically from the `drawBlock` to generate a random seed. This corrects a small security flaw we didn't address for simplicity's sake in SimpleLottery. The blockhash of the previous block is known to the user when they trigger the `drawWinner` function. If they see that the blockhash is going to give them the prize, they can keep waiting to trigger the function until they see a blockhash that will give them the prize. The only user with an incentive to trigger the function is the one who would receive the prize from that particular hash. So everybody would have to sit there running moduli on the blockhashes and triggering the function for their winning block so that a malicious actor doesn't take advantage of their laziness.

Specifying an exact block for the blockhash solves this problem. No matter when the `drawWinner` function is triggered, the same blockhash is used, so there is no advantage to waiting on the next block.

Unfortunately, this introduces another small worry for us to keep track of. Solidity and the EVM provide access to only the 256 most recent blockhashes. Anything older than that will return a value of 0x0. If the `drawWinner` function is not triggered within 256 blocks (~80 min) of the specified drawing block, the drawing will no longer be pseudorandom. Avoiding this flaw is thankfully simple. Make sure the lottery winner is drawn within an hour of the end of the lottery, and the flaw is no longer an issue.

The `counter` in the last line is actually the winning ticket. Because of the way our entries are stored, though, it ends up being used as a counter while determining the winning address (Listing 8-10), so that's why it has been named as such.

Listing 8-10. Calculating a RecurringLottery Round Winner

```
...
for (uint i=0; i < drawing.entries.length; i++) {
    uint quantity = drawing.entries[i].quantity;
    if (quantity > counter) {
        drawing.winner = drawing.entries[i].buyer;
        break;
    }
    elsea
        counter -= quantity;
}

balances[drawing.winner] += TICKET_PRICE *
                            drawing.entries.length;
...
```

Every entry has a quantity associated with it. The sum of the quantities in all entries, `drawing.totalQuantity`, was used to modulus the seed in Listing 8-9, and the result was stored in `counter`. This initial value of `counter` is the winning ticket, and we need to determine the address this ticket belongs to.

To do so, we loop through the entries and subtract the `quantity` of each entry from the `counter`. Eventually, we reach a point where the quantity of tickets in the entry is greater than the number left in the counter. This means one of the tickets in that entry must be the winning ticket, so we can mark the `buyer` of the entry as the winner and break out of the loop.

The prize is determined by multiplying the ticket price by the number of tickets sold in the round. It is credited to the user's balance for them to withdraw. The contract uses a standard withdraw function (see "Withdraw Methods" in Chapter 5).

Cleanup and Deployment

After a round is complete and the user has been paid out, the state for that round is no longer required. Because this state can be quite large if the contract becomes popular, a deleteRound function is provided so that we can be good blockchain citizens and clean up old data (Listing 8-11).

Listing 8-11. Deleting Old Round State

```
function deleteRound (uint _round) public {
    require(block.number > rounds[_round].drawBlock + 100);
    require(rounds[_round].winner != address(0));
    delete rounds[_round];
}
```

If it has been more than 100 blocks since the drawing block and the winner has already been drawn, this function deletes the specified round. Anyone can call this function.

The migration for this contract is similar to SimpleLottery. A duration is specified in blocks instead of seconds. The full migration is available at the GitHub repo at https://github.com/k26dr/ethereum-games/blob/master/migrations/10_recurring_lottery.js. Only the two nonstandard lines are printed in Listing 8-12.

Listing 8-12. RecurringLottery Migration

```
// duration is in blocks. 1 day = ~5500 blocks
var duration = 5500 * 7; // 7 days
deployer.deploy(RecurringLottery, duration);
```

We've set the round duration to approximately seven days in our migration and the deployed contracts in Exercise 8-2, but feel free to modify it for your own use.

EXERCISE 8-2. PLAY THE LOTTERY

We have deployed our RecurringLottery to both the mainnet (`https://etherscan.io/address/0x9283340ee8f47b59511a4f1a4bad3c5466283c09`) and the testnet (`https://rinkeby.etherscan.io/address/0x6d198b8c429da4536f2b77d3b92731e025207884`) if you wish to play. Buy a ticket and try your luck. While you wait on the weekly lottery draw, check whether there are any undrawn rounds or rounds that can be deleted. If there are, do your fellow readers a service and run the transactions required to draw or delete the rounds.

RNG Lottery

Using a blockhash as the source of entropy for RNG has its theoretical limits. If the ether prize for the lottery greatly exceeds the block reward, the miners become incentivized to manipulate the blockhashes in their favor, discarding any valid hashes they create that don't award them the prize.

At the moment, this attack vector is merely theoretical. No one has exploited it with any sort of success. In the case of a lottery with hundreds of tickets, a miner could improve their odds only by a few percentage points by discarding hashes. However, a more secure RNG using lotteries has been proposed and is worth covering here.

Because the purpose of this contract is to demonstrate the use of a more secure RNG, we will keep the lottery functionality simple. It will be a nonrecurring lottery with only single-ticket purchases.

The idea behind the RNG lottery is to use a commit-reveal sequence to create a verifiably random number. Every buyer submits a commitment hash when they buy a ticket. The commitment is generated by hashing together the user's address and a secret number known only to the user.

When the ticketing period is over, there is a reveal period during which each player must reveal the secret number used to generate their commitment hash. The secret number is hashed on-chain with the player's address, and this hash must match the commitment submitted with the ticket. Players who don't reveal their numbers during the reveal period are dropped from the lottery. The secret numbers are hashed together to generate the random seed for picking a winner.

Listing 8-13 lists the whole contract before we explore the contract in detail.

Listing 8-13. RNG Lottery

```
contract RNGLottery {
    uint constant public TICKET_PRICE = 1e16;

    address[] public tickets;
    address public winner;
    bytes32 public seed;
    mapping(address => bytes32) public commitments;

    uint public ticketDeadline;
    uint public revealDeadline;
    uint public drawBlock;

    function RNGLottery (uint duration,
      uint revealDuration) public {
        ticketDeadline = block.number + duration;
        revealDeadline = ticketDeadline + revealDuration;
        drawBlock = revealDeadline + 5;
    }

    function createCommitment(address user, uint N)
      public pure returns (bytes32 commitment) {
        return keccak256(user, N);
    }
```

```
function buy (bytes32 commitment) payable public {
    require(msg.value == TICKET_PRICE);
    require(block.number <= ticketDeadline);

    commitments[msg.sender] = commitment;
}

function reveal (uint N) public {
    require(block.number > ticketDeadline);
    require(block.number <= revealDeadline);

    bytes32 hash = createCommitment(msg.sender, N);
    require(hash == commitments[msg.sender]);

    seed = keccak256(seed, N);
    tickets.push(msg.sender);
}

function drawWinner () public {
    require(block.number > drawBlock);
    require(winner == address(0));

    uint randIndex = uint(seed) % tickets.length;
    winner = tickets[randIndex];
}

function withdraw () public {
    require(msg.sender == winner);
    msg.sender.transfer(this.balance);
}
}
```

This contract has four new variables that you haven't seen before:

- seed: This is the random seed we will use to determine a winner. Each time a secret number is revealed, the seed is modified to incorporate the reveal.

- commitments: Every player submits a commitment with their ticket purchase. This mapping stores those commitments.

- ticketDeadline: The equivalent of endBlock from earlier contracts. Tickets cannot be purchased after this block number.

- revealDeadline: The reveal phase is new and requires a deadline as well. All reveals must occur after the ticket deadline and before the reveal deadline.

The constructor takes two duration parameters instead of one this time (one for the ticketing period and one for the reveal period) and uses the durations to set deadlines for the ticket and reveal periods.

Before purchasing a ticket, a user must first create a commitment. To make this easy for the user, the contract contains a createCommitment function (Listing 8-14).

Listing 8-14. Solidity Function for Creating a Commitment

```
function createCommitment(address user, uint N)
  public pure returns (bytes32 commitment) {
    return keccak256(user, N);
}
```

This function uses an address and a secret number, N, to create a commitment hash. The address should be the user's address so that the commitment can be verified properly on-chain during the reveal phase.

The user's address is concatenated to the secret number before the hash for the same reason salts are used in password storage. Using just the number exposes the commitment to a dictionary attack. An attacker can maintain a large database containing hashes of common numbers, phrases, or byte sequences. If the secret number ends up being a common number, an attacker could determine the number from the hash. Prepending the user address to the number before hashing makes it highly unlikely that the hash will be available in a database.

This is the first time we've had a use for a pure function. The output of a pure function depends solely on the function arguments. Because of this, calling a pure function does not require sending a transaction. The result can be calculated and used locally without having to update the state tree and go through the consensus protocol. A user can generate a commitment locally in the Truffle dev console (Listing 8-15).

Listing 8-15. Creating a Commitment Locally

```
lottery = RNGLottery.at(RNGLottery.address)
N = 173849032
lottery.createCommitment(web3.eth.accounts[0], N)
```

The third line will spit out the commitment as a 32-byte hex string. This commitment can then be used in a ticket purchase transaction (Listing 8-16).

Listing 8-16. Purchasing a Ticket with a Commitment

```
commitment = lottery.createCommitment(
  web3.eth.accounts[0], N)
lottery.buy(commitment,
  { from: web3.eth.accounts[0], value: 1e16 })
```

> **Note**   If you are interested in seeing a more in-depth interaction
> with multiple commits and reveals, a full test interaction is available
> on the GitHub repo at `test/RNGLottery.js`.

The ticket purchase logic is simple (Listing 8-17). It verifies that the
proper value was sent with the transaction and that that the ticket deadline
hasn't passed, and stores the commitment for later use.

Listing 8-17. RNG Lottery Ticket Purchase Logic

```
function buy (bytes32 commitment) payable public {
    require(msg.value == TICKET_PRICE);
    require(block.number <= ticketDeadline);

    commitments[msg.sender] = commitment;
}
```

The reveal logic is more interesting (Listing 8-18).

Listing 8-18. Revealing and Verifying Secret Numbers

```
function reveal (uint N) public {
    require(block.number > ticketDeadline);
    require(block.number <= revealDeadline);

    bytes32 hash = createCommitment(msg.sender, N);
    require(hash == commitments[msg.sender]);

    seed = keccak256(seed, N);
    tickets.push(msg.sender);
}
```

The function takes one argument: the secret number N being revealed. The first two checks ensure that the current block is in the reveal period. Then a commitment hash is created from the revealed number and user address, using the same function as in the commit phase to avoid errors from differences in implementation. This generated hash must match the hash from the commitment exactly, or the function will throw an error.

To generate an updated seed, the secret number is concatenated to the current seed, and the hash of the concatenated byte sequence is stored as the new seed. In this way, each reveal updates the seed with its own secret number until all players have modified the seed.

The beauty of this system is that it requires only one honest actor to succeed. A single unknown reveal is enough to make it impossible to predict the final generated seed. This means players don't have to trust each other to ensure a fair outcome. Each player has to ensure only that their own number is kept secret. To predict the outcome, an attacker would have to know every secret number, the order in which they will be revealed, and the total number of tickets that will be purchased.

The remainder of the code, the drawWinner and withdraw functions, are nearly identical to SimpleLottery, so we do not discuss them further here.

The migration for the RNG lottery is slightly different from the other lotteries because it takes two arguments instead of one. Only the differing lines are reproduced in Listing 8-19. The full migration is available on the GitHub repo at https://github.com/k26dr/ethereum-games/blob/master/migrations/11_rng_lottery.js.

Listing 8-19. Deploying the RNG Lottery

```
// duration is in blocks. 1 day = ~5500 blocks
var duration = 5500 * 7; // 7 days
var revealDuration = 5500 * 3; // 3 days
deployer.deploy(RNGLottery, duration, revealDuration);
```

Powerball

Powerball is the most popular type of lottery played in the United States. In this section, we are going to write a contract that ports this game onto Ethereum.

In Powerball, the user picks six numbers per ticket. The first five numbers are standard numbers from 1–69, and the sixth number is a special Powerball number from 1–26 that offers extra rewards. Every three or four days, a drawing is held, and a winning ticket consisting of five standard numbers and a Powerball number is picked. Prizes are paid out based on the number of winning numbers matched on your ticket.

Figure 8-2 reproduces the payouts and odds from the official Powerball site (`www.powerball.com/powerball/pb_prizes.asp`). The Grand Prize refers to the full jackpot, which in our case will be the full balance of the contract.

Match	Prize	Odds
●●●●● + BALL	Grand Prize	1 in 292,201,338.00
●●●●●	$1,000,000	1 in 11,688,053.52
●●●● + BALL	$50,000	1 in 913,129.18
●●●●	$100	1 in 36,525.17
●●● + BALL	$100	1 in 14,494.11
●●●	$7	1 in 579.76
●● + BALL	$7	1 in 701.33
● + BALL	$4	1 in 91.98
BALL	$4	1 in 38.32

The overall odds of winning a prize are 1 in 24.87.
The odds presented here are based on a $2 play (rounded to two decimal places).

Figure 8-2. *Powerball win criteria, odds, and payouts*

The code for the full Powerball contract is displayed in Listing 8-20.

Listing 8-20. Powerball Smart Contract

```
contract Powerball {
    struct Round {
        uint endTime;
        uint drawBlock;
        uint[6] winningNumbers;
        mapping(address => uint[6][]) tickets;
    }
```

```
uint public constant TICKET_PRICE = 2e15;
uint public constant MAX_NUMBER = 69;
uint public constant MAX_POWERBALL_NUMBER = 26;
uint public constant ROUND_LENGTH = 3 days;

uint public round;
mapping(uint => Round) public rounds;

function Powerball () public {
    round = 1;
    rounds[round].endTime = now + ROUND_LENGTH;
}

function buy (uint[6][] numbers) payable public {
    require(numbers.length * TICKET_PRICE == msg.value);

    for (uint i=0; i < numbers.length; i++) {
        for (uint j=0; j < 6; j++)
            require(numbers[i][j] > 0);
        for (j=0; j < 5; j++)
            require(numbers[i][j] <= MAX_NUMBER);
            require(numbers[i][5] <= MAX_POWERBALL_NUMBER);
    }

    // check for round expiry
    if (now > rounds[round].endTime) {
        rounds[round].drawBlock = block.number + 5;
        round += 1;
        rounds[round].endTime = now + ROUND_LENGTH;
    }

    for (i=0; i < numbers.length; i++)
        rounds[round].tickets[msg.sender].push(numbers[i]);
}
```

```solidity
function drawNumbers (uint _round) public {
    uint drawBlock = rounds[_round].drawBlock;
    require(now > rounds[_round].endTime);
    require(block.number >= drawBlock);
    require(rounds[_round].winningNumbers[0] == 0);

    for (uint i=0; i < 5; i++) {
        bytes32 rand = keccak256(block.blockhash(drawBlock), i);
        uint numberDraw = uint(rand) % MAX_NUMBER + 1;
        rounds[_round].winningNumbers[i] = numberDraw;
    }
    rand = keccak256(block.blockhash(drawBlock), uint(5));
    uint powerballDraw = uint(rand) % MAX_POWERBALL_NUMBER + 1;
    rounds[_round].winningNumbers[5] = powerballDraw;
}
function claim (uint _round) public {
    require(rounds[_round].tickets[msg.sender].length > 0);
    require(rounds[_round].winningNumbers[0] != 0);

    uint[6][] storage myNumbers = rounds[_round].
    tickets[msg.sender];
    uint[6] storage winningNumbers = rounds[_round].
    winningNumbers;

    uint payout = 0;
    for (uint i=0; i < myNumbers.length; i++) {
        uint numberMatches = 0;
        for (uint j=0; j < 5; j++) {
            for (uint k=0; k < 5; k++) {
                if (myNumbers[i][j] == winningNumbers[k])
                    numberMatches += 1;
            }
```

```
        }
        bool powerballMatches =
          (myNumbers[i][5] == winningNumbers[5]);

        // win conditions
        if (numberMatches == 5 && powerballMatches) {
            payout = this.balance;
            break;
        }
        else if (numberMatches == 5)
            payout += 1000 ether;
        else if (numberMatches == 4 && powerballMatches)
            payout += 50 ether;
        else if (numberMatches == 4)
            payout += 1e17; // .1 ether
        else if (numberMatches == 3 && powerballMatches)
            payout += 1e17; // .1 ether
        else if (numberMatches == 3)
            payout += 7e15; // .007 ether
        else if (numberMatches == 2 && powerballMatches)
            payout += 7e15; // .007 ether
        else if (powerballMatches)
            payout += 4e15; // .004 ether
    }

    msg.sender.transfer(payout);
    delete rounds[_round].tickets[msg.sender];
}

function ticketsFor(uint _round, address user) public view
  returns (uint[6][] tickets) {
    return rounds[_round].tickets[user];
}
```

```
function winningNumbersFor(uint _round) public view
  returns (uint[6] winningNumbers) {
    return rounds[_round].winningNumbers;
  }
}
```

This is the most complex of the lotteries in this chapter. It is a recurring lottery with multiticket purchases and multiple payouts.

The Round struct is similar to the one from the recurring lottery. Each round has a ticket purchase deadline endTime, a future block number drawBlock to use for generating a random number, an array of six winningNumbers, and a mapping of user addresses to tickets. A ticket consists of six numbers chosen by a player while buying a ticket. Because a single player can have multiple tickets, the data type of the tickets is uint[6][].

As a reminder, Solidity multidimensional array syntax is the opposite of Java and C. In Solidity, uint[6][] refers to a dynamic array of uint[6] elements, not a six-element array of uint[]. A list of three tickets would take the shape of Listing 8-21.

Listing 8-21. Multidimensional Ticket Array

```
tickets = [
    [1, 2, 3, 4, 5, 6],
    [10, 2, 31, 43, 37, 15],
    [60, 15, 14, 12, 1, 6]
]
```

We define four constants for use in the contract:

- TICKET_PRICE: The price of a single ticket. Set to .002 ether.

- MAX_NUMBER: This is the maximum number permitted while picking ticket numbers. We will be following the official Powerball rules, which sets this to 69.

- MAX_POWERBALL_NUMBER: The Powerball number has a more constricted range than the first five standard numbers. Official Powerball rules set this to 26.

- ROUND_LENGTH: The length of a round in seconds. This is set to 3 days for the full game, but the test script provided later in the chapter requires this to be set to 15 seconds for speedier rounds.

Because the majority of the complexity is contained in the Round struct, we have only two state variables:

- round: The current round number. Tickets bought for a round are matched against only the winning numbers for that round.

- rounds: A mapping from round numbers to Round structs.

The constructor function is similarly simple, and we do not reproduce it here. It starts the lottery by setting the round to 1 and setting the endTime for the round ROUND_LENGTH seconds in the future.

There are three state-modifying functions in the contract and two additional view functions to make it easier for users to read the contract state. The first of these is the buy function. The first half of the buy function performs a series of checks on the input data (Listing 8-22).

Listing 8-22. Powerball Ticket Purchase Requirements

```
function buy (uint[6][] numbers) payable public {
    require(numbers.length * TICKET_PRICE == msg.value);

    for (uint i=0; i < numbers.length; i++) {
        for (uint j=0; j < 6; j++)
            require(numbers[i][j] > 0);
```

```
    for (j=0; j < 5; j++)
        require(numbers[i][j] <= MAX_NUMBER);
    require(numbers[i][5] <= MAX_POWERBALL_NUMBER);
}
...
```

In order to buy a ticket, the user must pass in a list of ticket numbers similar to those in Listing 8-20. The code in Listing 8-22 verifies that the appropriate amount of ether has been passed for the number of ticket submissions. It then loops through the tickets and verifies that each of them has selected numbers in an appropriate range. Standard numbers must be in the range of 1–69, and Powerball numbers must be in the range of 1–26.

If the tickets pass inspection, the second half of the buy function updates the contract state with the tickets (Listing 8-23).

Listing 8-23. Ticket Purchase Logic

```
// check for round expiry
if (now > rounds[round].endTime) {
    rounds[round].drawBlock = block.number + 5;
    round += 1;
    rounds[round].endTime = now + ROUND_LENGTH;
}

for (i=0; i < numbers.length; i++)
    rounds[round].tickets[msg.sender].push(numbers[i]);
}
```

First, round update logic must be handled. If the current round has expired, a `drawBlock` is set for that round, `round` is incremented, and an `endTime` is set for the new round.

This logic has a small flaw that should be addressed. The `drawBlock` for a round is not set until the first ticket of the next round is purchased. In theory, the drawing for a round could be delayed forever if no one purchases a ticket for the next round. In practice, we expect the lottery to be continuous and not run into this issue. In the worst-case scenario, someone could simply purchase a ticket for the next round to trigger a drawing.

Once the round has been determined, the tickets are pushed one by one into the user's ticket pool for that round.

When a round is complete and its `drawBlock` has passed, the `drawNumbers` function can be called for that round. This function randomly draws six numbers that serve as the winning ticket for that round. The first half of the function runs a series of checks to make sure the numbers are drawn only once at the appropriate time (Listing 8-24).

Listing 8-24. Time and State Checks Before Drawing Numbers

```
function drawNumbers (uint _round) public {
    uint drawBlock = rounds[_round].drawBlock;
    require(now > rounds[_round].endTime);
    require(block.number >= drawBlock);
    require(rounds[_round].winningNumbers[0] == 0);
    ...
```

This block of code verifies that the round has ended, the `drawBlock` has passed, and the winning numbers haven't already been set. Unset numbers are always zero, and the winning numbers can never be zero, so just checking the first winning number is enough to know whether the winning ticket has already been drawn.

It seems redundant to require that the round has ended when we are also checking that `drawBlock` has passed. We include both checks because `drawBlock` is not set until the end of a round. An unset `uint` has a value of zero, so that check is insufficient during a round; hence, we run a check against the round's `endTime` as well.

The winning numbers are drawn randomly from the set of valid numbers (Listing 8-25).

Listing 8-25. Drawing Winning Powerball Numbers

```
for (uint i=0; i < 5; i++) {
    bytes32 rand = keccak256(block.blockhash(drawBlock),i);
    uint numberDraw = uint(rand) % MAX_NUMBER + 1;
    rounds[_round].winningNumbers[i] = numberDraw;
}
rand = keccak256(block.blockhash(drawBlock), uint(5));
uint powerballDraw = uint(rand) % MAX_POWERBALL_NUMBER + 1;
rounds[_round].winningNumbers[5] = powerballDraw;
```

This is a pretty complex piece of logic, but it simplifies when you realize that the last three lines are mostly a repeat of the three lines inside the for loop.

This code generates a random number, uses a modulus to bound the range of the random numbers, and then stores the generated number as one of the winning numbers. Keep in mind that Solidity stores only the 256 most recent blockhashes, so this logic must be executed within 256 blocks (~80 min) of the drawBlock.

When generating a random number, we can't simply reuse the same blockhash every time, because we would end up with the same number repeated five times. Instead, we concatenate a unique number (in this case, i) to the blockhash each time, and hash the resulting byte string to get our seed.

The difference between the five iterations inside the for loop and the one outside is the number used for the modulus. The first five numbers are standard numbers from 1–69 and use MAX_NUMBER for the modulus. The final number, the Powerball number, is restricted to the range 1–26 and uses MAX_POWERBALL_NUMBER for the modulus. Both versions add 1 to the modulus output to prevent 0 from being drawn.

After the numbers have been drawn, any user with a winning ticket can claim their rewards for the round. The first part of the claim function performs some checks and declares the necessary variables (Listing 8-26).

Listing 8-26. Claiming Powerball Rewards: Checks and Variables

```
function claim (uint _round) public {
    require(rounds[_round].tickets[msg.sender].length > 0);
    require(rounds[_round].winningNumbers[0] != 0);

    uint[6][] storage myNumbers =
        rounds[_round].tickets[msg.sender];
    uint[6] storage winningNumbers =
        rounds[_round].winningNumbers;

    uint payout = 0;
    ...
```

The function takes a round number as an argument. Tickets from one round are not valid in another round. The user must have bought tickets in the specified round, and the winning numbers for the round must have been drawn already in order to claim rewards.

The user's tickets and the winning numbers for the round are pulled from the state tree to myNumbers and winningNumbers. The total reward paid out to the user will be tracked with payout.

Next, we count the number of matches between the user's numbers and the winning numbers (Listing 8-27).

Listing 8-27. Claiming Powerball Rewards: Counting Matches

```
for (uint i=0; i < myNumbers.length; i++) {
    uint numberMatches = 0;
    for (uint j=0; j < 5; j++) {
        for (uint k=0; k < 5; k++) {
```

```
            if (myNumbers[i][j] == winningNumbers[k])
                numberMatches += 1;
        }
    }
    bool powerballMatches =
      (myNumbers[i][5] == winningNumbers[5]);
    ...
```

The outermost loop (using i) is a loop through the user's tickets. Each ticket has an individual set of six numbers, so each ticket must be evaluated separately. The two inner loops (using j and k) compare the ticket's first five numbers (standard numbers) to the winning standard numbers and count the number of matches. The order of the standard numbers does not matter in Powerball, so a match against any of the standard winning numbers is counted. Matches between a Powerball number and a standard number are not counted.

After the standard numbers are compared, the ticket's Powerball number is compared directly to the winning Powerball number. When this is complete, payouts can be made based on the number and type of matches (Listing 8-28).

Listing 8-28. Claiming Powerball Rewards: Calculating Payouts

```
// win conditions
if (numberMatches == 5 && powerballMatches) {
    payout = this.balance;
    break;
}
else if (numberMatches == 5)
    payout += 1000 ether;
else if (numberMatches == 4 && powerballMatches)
    payout += 50 ether;
```

```
else if (numberMatches == 4)
    payout += 1e17; // .1 ether
else if (numberMatches == 3 && powerballMatches)
    payout += 1e17; // .1 ether
else if (numberMatches == 3)
    payout += 7e15; // .007 ether
else if (numberMatches == 2 && powerballMatches)
    payout += 4e15; // .004 ether
else if (powerballMatches)
    payout += 4e15; // .004 ether
```

These payouts are pulled directly from the rules in Figure 8-2. This block of code is contained within the outermost for loop (using i) from Listing 8-27 and executes once for each ticket. The final value of payout will be the sum of the winnings from each ticket.

The one exception to this rule occurs on the rare chance that a user hits the jackpot and matches all five numbers plus the Powerball. In that case, we break out of the loop and hand the user the full balance of the contract. If we attempted to use the standard payout logic with a jackpot, we might accidentally run into a situation where the user also has another ticket that earns a payout. In this case, we would end up trying to pay out something like this.balance + .004 ether, which would be greater than the balance of the contract and throw an error due to insufficient funds. The user would have somehow magically hit the jackpot and not be able to claim it.

After calculating the payout, we attempt to send the payout to the user:

```
msg.sender.transfer(payout);
delete rounds[_round].tickets[msg.sender];
```

If the payout goes through successfully, we delete the user's tickets so that they can't attempt to claim their prize again.

There's one catch to the payout. It can occur only if the contract has enough ether to make the payout. Unlike a traditional lottery, in which the lottery is funded by an initial investor who backs the prizes, our decentralized lottery can pay out only a prize that has been paid to it with ticket purchases. If you match five numbers and the contract doesn't have 1,000 ether, you must wait until the contract has 1,000 ether to claim your prize. You can claim your prize at any time and attempt to claim your prize as many times as you want, so you will never lose your potential reward.

The remaining functions in the contract are view functions for reading the contract state (Listing 8-29).

Listing 8-29. Viewing Powerball Tickets and Winning Numbers

```
function ticketsFor(uint _round, address user) public view
  returns (uint[6][] tickets) {
    return rounds[_round].tickets[user];
}

function winningNumbersFor(uint _round) public view
  returns (uint[6] winningNumbers) {
    return rounds[_round].winningNumbers;
}
```

For a public struct, Solidity will automatically generate a getter function. This getter will return a list of items corresponding to the variables in the struct in their order of declaration. However, Solidity will not include complex data types in the returned array. For mappings and arrays, we must generate our own view functions. Figure 8-3 shows the expected output from calling the .rounds() getter.

```
truffle(develop)> lottery = Powerball.at(Powerball.address);
truffle(develop)> lottery.rounds(1)
[ { [String: '1514340760'] s: 1, e: 9, c: [ 1514340760 ] },
  { [String: '0'] s: 1, e: 0, c: [ 0 ] } ]
```

Figure 8-3. *Viewing Powerball round structs*

There are two fields in the returned JavaScript array corresponding to endTime and drawBlock. The other two fields, winningNumbers and tickets, are not displayed because they are complex data types. The two view functions in Listing 8-29 allow us to read these otherwise unreadable states.

We have covered the details of the contract, but we have not covered exactly how to interact with the contract. Doing so is left as an exercise for you. A standard migration for deploying the contract is available on the GitHub repo at https://github.com/k26dr/ethereum-games/blob/master/migrations/12_powerball.js. We expect you will be able to run a sample interaction on your own, but if you get stuck, a test interaction is available at https://github.com/k26dr/ethereum-games/blob/master/test/powerball.js. When you feel comfortable with the contract, you can play on the mainnet in Exercise 8-3.

EXERCISE 8-3. POWERBALLING

Play the Powerball lottery and win big prizes! Millionaires are minted every day—only two finney to play! Come one, come all! Get your savings and throw them down the drain! For novices, we have Powerball on the testnet (https://rinkeby.etherscan.io/address/0x274c0f91642acbe737 d10c9ceddeb1b500caf39b). For our true high rollers we have Powerball on the Ethereum mainnet (https://etherscan.io/address/0xcab5fb317 667978e5c428393ddf98a5dc4bc15dc).

(P.S. If you still think playing the lottery is a good deal after this, run the test script that buys 500 tickets at a time and watch how little you get back in winnings.)

Summary

In this chapter, we slowly progressed from writing simple lotteries to writing the most complex contract we've written to date, Powerball. We included a lot of niche Solidity features into our contracts for the first time, including multidimensional arrays, `view` functions, and `pure` functions. We spent a considerable amount of time perfecting our use of random numbers with blockhashes and commit-reveal lotteries. In the next chapter, we will take a break from scams and gambling to cover prize puzzles.

CHAPTER 9

Prize Puzzles

Prize puzzles are a unique use case for smart contracts and a great example of blockchains unlocking new functionality. The idea behind a prize puzzle is for a benefactor to put up a bounty for answering a question, using a smart contract to verifiably lock up the reward so that only the correct answer can unlock the contract.

In this chapter, we will create two types of prize puzzles: a simple puzzle that unlocks immediately when the answer is provided and a commit-reveal style puzzle that permits multiple winners. We will then present a couple of prize puzzles that we have posted to the mainnet and invite you to take a shot at claiming the rewards.

Before getting into the code, however, we have to cover the basics of answer obfuscation.

Obscuring Answers

The security of a prize puzzle rests on its ability to obscure the answer from players. Because all data in a smart contract is public, the answer in some form must rest on the blockchain without leaking its exact contents. Updating the contract with the answer after players have submitted guesses is a less-than-ideal option because the contract creator could change the answer after the players have submitted guesses.

© Kedar Iyer and Chris Dannen 2018
K. Iyer and C. Dannen, *Building Games with Ethereum Smart Contracts*,
https://doi.org/10.1007/978-1-4842-3492-1_9

We will be using the following simple hash scheme to obscure our answers in the contract. Before creating the contract, the creator must hash the answer with their address to produce a commitment. The address acts as a salt that makes cracking the hash virtually impossible. The commitment is then submitted along with a bounty during contract creation and stored in the contract.

For the simple puzzle, players submit their guesses directly to the contract, which then uses the salt to hash the guess and compare it to the commitment. If the hash matches the commitment, the prize is unlocked.

In the commit-reveal puzzle, players create their own commitments off-chain by hashing their address with their guess and then submit the commitment to the chain. The creator then reveals the answer, and any player who reveals a correct guess during the reveal period gets a share of the prize.

Simple Puzzle

For our simple puzzle, let's set up the following question as the prize (Listing 9-1).

Listing 9-1. A Simple Puzzle

If we list all the natural numbers below 10 that are multiples of 3 or 5, we get 3, 5, 6, and 9. The sum of these multiples is 23.

Find the sum of all the multiples of 3 or 5 below 1,000.

This question is from the Project Euler questions page at https://projecteuler.net/problem=1 if you're interested in solving more like it.

We want to create a contract that unlocks ether when the correct answer is guessed. Listing 9-2 displays a simple contract that will do so.

Listing 9-2. Simple Prize Puzzle

```
contract SimplePrize {
    bytes32 public constant salt = bytes32(987463829);
    bytes32 public commitment;

    function SimplePrize(bytes32 _commitment)
      public payable {
        commitment = _commitment;
    }

    function createCommitment(uint answer)
      public view returns (bytes32) {
        return keccak256(salt, answer);
    }

    function guess (uint answer) public {
        require(createCommitment(answer) == commitment);
        msg.sender.transfer(this.balance);
    }

    function () public payable {}
}
```

This contract has one constant and only one state variable:

- salt: A long byte string to prepend to hashes. Used to prevent attackers from guessing the answer with a dictionary attack. Any random byte string will be adequate as a salt. We kept ours small so it would fit on the page, but ideally it would be a full 32-byte string.

- commitment: The byte string created by hashing the salt and the answer together. Used to verify guesses without revealing the answer.

The logic of the contract is fairly simple and straightforward. The constructor function stores the provided commitment for later use. The createCommitment function is the same as the one from the RNG lottery in Chapter 8.

Both the constructor and fallback functions are payable so that the prize can be funded. Our migration will be funding the contract on creation, but it can be funded at any time by sending ether to the contract's address as well. This way, multiple addresses can fund a single prize if they have an interest in doing so.

The guess function (Listing 9-3) determines whether a proposed answer is correct.

Listing 9-3. Guessing Answers for a Simple Prize

```
function guess (uint answer) public {
    require(createCommitment(answer) == commitment);
    msg.sender.transfer(this.balance);
}
```

Using the same function used to create the original commitment, a hash is computed from the answer and salt. If the hash matches the stored commitment, the user is sent the full balance of the contract. The answer is public, and anybody can view the winning submission if they wish to verify the answer themselves.

Deploying the contract is the complex part of this contract. We have a chicken-and-egg problem in front of us. To create a commitment, we need a contract, but to create a contract, we need a commitment. We solve this issue by first deploying a contract with a bogus commitment. The migration for the contract can be found on the GitHub repo at https://github.com/k26dr/ethereum-games/blob/master/migrations/13_simple_prize.js. Just the relevant portions are reproduced in Listing 9-4.

Listing 9-4. Deploying the Simple Prize Contract

```
//deployer.deploy(SimplePrize, "0x0"); // use this to generate
                                        commitment
deployer.deploy(SimplePrize,
"0x9e85ce2a4f5c2955f54aa61046f6f13b096d025166f03b5dd7faacc3e1e8f07e",
{ value: 1e16 });
```

The migration contains two separate deployment statements. The first one is the dummy deployment, which will allow us to create the commitment. The second one is the true prize puzzle deployment with a proper answer. The first line is intentionally commented out to show that only one of them is used at a time.

For the first line, we will uncomment the first line and comment out the second deploy statement. The migration will run the following code only:

deployer.deploy(SimplePrize, "0x0");

To deploy the contract and create a commitment, run the code in Listing 9-5 one line at a time in the dev console. The code assumes that migration 13 contains the SimplePrize deployment code.

Listing 9-5. Creating a Commitment

```
migrate -f 13
prize = SimplePrize.at(SimplePrize.address)
prize.createCommitment(42)
```

The final line will spit out a hash that corresponds to our commitment. This is the commitment we will use to deploy the real version of our contract.

There's a catch, though. If you check the real commitment in Listing 9-4 against the commitment generated by Listing 9-5, you will see that they don't match. That's because we didn't give you the real answer in Listing 9-5! Instead, you're going to deploy the contract in Exercise 9-1 and figure out the answer yourself.

EXERCISE 9-1. MAKE EULER PROUD

Deploy the SimplePrize contract to the dev console by using
`migrations/13_simple_prize`. The contract contains a prize you can
unlock by solving the puzzle given in Listing 9-1. Solve the puzzle and use
the dev console to unlock the prize. You will know your guess is correct if the
transaction returns a receipt. Wrong answers will throw an error.

Commit-Reveal Puzzle

In a *commit-reveal puzzle*, each user has a chance to make a guess before
the answer is revealed. The prize is then split among all the users who
guess right. For our commit-reveal puzzle example, we will use the second
question from Project Euler (`https://projecteuler.net/problem=2`); see
Listing 9-6.

Listing 9-6. Commit-Reveal Puzzle Question

Each new term in the Fibonacci sequence is generated by adding
the previous two terms. By starting with 1 and 2, the first 10
terms will be as follows:

    1, 2, 3, 5, 8, 13, 21, 34, 55, 89, ...

By considering the terms in the Fibonacci sequence whose values
do not exceed 4 million, find the sum of the even-valued terms.

As usual, we will produce the full contract in Listing 9-7 and discuss
specifics later.

Listing 9-7. Commit-Reveal Puzzle Contract

```
contract CommitRevealPuzzle {
    uint public constant GUESS_DURATION_BLOCKS = 5; // 3 days
    uint public constant REVEAL_DURATION_BLOCKS = 5; // 1 day

    address public creator;
    uint public guessDeadline;
    uint public revealDeadline;
    uint public totalPrize;
    mapping(address => bytes32) public commitments;
    address[] public winners;
    mapping(address => bool) public claimed;

    function CommitRevealPuzzle(bytes32 _commitment) public
    payable {
        creator = msg.sender;
        commitments[creator] = _commitment;
        guessDeadline = block.number + GUESS_DURATION_BLOCKS;
        revealDeadline = guessDeadline + REVEAL_DURATION_BLOCKS;
        totalPrize += msg.value;
    }

    function createCommitment(address user, uint answer)
      public pure returns (bytes32) {
        return keccak256(user, answer);
    }

    function guess(bytes32 _commitment) public {
        require(block.number < guessDeadline);
        require(msg.sender != creator);
        commitments[msg.sender] = _commitment;
    }
```

```
function reveal(uint answer) public {
    require(block.number > guessDeadline);
    require(block.number < revealDeadline);
    require(createCommitment(msg.sender, answer) ==
            commitments[msg.sender]);
    require(createCommitment(creator, answer) ==
            commitments[creator]);
    require(!isWinner(msg.sender));

    winners.push(msg.sender);
}

function claim () public {
    require(block.number > revealDeadline);
    require(claimed[msg.sender] == false);
    require(isWinner(msg.sender));

    uint payout = totalPrize / winners.length;
    claimed[msg.sender] = true;
    msg.sender.transfer(payout);
}

function isWinner (address user) public view returns (bool) {
    bool winner = false;
    for (uint i=0; i < winners.length; i++) {
        if (winners[i] == user) {
            winner = true;
            break;
        }
    }
    return winner;
}
```

```
function () public payable {
    totalPrize += msg.value;
}
}
```

This contract is much more complex than our simple prize puzzle. The contract is split into guessing, revealing, and claiming periods, each with its own function. Let's step through the state variables and constants:

- GUESS_DURATION_BLOCKS: The duration of the guessing period in blocks. We will set this number low for testing and at 16,500 (three days) for a real deployment.

- REVEAL_DURATION_BLOCKS: The duration of the reveal period. Standard is 5,500 blocks (1 day), but we will set this lower for testing.

- creator: The creator of the contract.

- guessDeadline: The block number corresponding to the end of the guessing period.

- revealDeadline: The block number corresponding to the end of the reveal period.

- totalPrize: The value of the prize in wei. This needs to be tracked because the balance of the contract changes as each winner withdraws their prize.

- commitments: A mapping from user addresses to the commitments they submit with their guess.

- winners: List of winning addresses.

- claimed: As winners claim their share of the prize, we will mark their share as claimed by using this mapping.

The constructor requires a commitment created from hashing the creator's address with the puzzle answer to be included on contract creation (Listing 9-8).

Listing 9-8. Commit-Reveal Puzzle Constructor

```
function CommitRevealPuzzle(bytes32 _commitment)
  public payable {
    creator = msg.sender;
    commitments[creator] = _commitment;
    guessDeadline = block.number + GUESS_DURATION_BLOCKS;
    revealDeadline = guessDeadline +
                     REVEAL_DURATION_BLOCKS;
    totalPrize += msg.value;
}
```

The commitment is generated off-chain by passing the contract creator's address and the puzzle answer to the `createCommitment` function. See the "Simple Puzzle" section previously in this chapter, and the "RNG Lottery" section in Chapter 8 for details on generating the commitment.

The constructor sets deadlines, stores the answer commitment, and adds any ether passed with the message to the prize. The prize can be increased at any point by sending more ether to the contract. The fallback function is `payable` and adds the ether sent to the total prize.

The `guess` function requires a similar commitment, this time from the player (Listing 9-9).

Listing 9-9. Submitting a Guess to Commit-Reveal Puzzle

```
function guess(bytes32 _commitment) public {
    require(block.number < guessDeadline);
    require(msg.sender != creator);
    commitments[msg.sender] = _commitment;
}
```

The function verifies that the guessing deadline has not passed, and more important, that the sender is not the creator. Because we store the answer to the puzzle in the commitments mapping along with the guesses, allowing the creator to guess would be the equivalent of allowing the creator to change the answer to the puzzle.

The reveal function runs a series of checks and adds the player to the winners array if the submission passes all the checks (Listing 9-10).

Listing 9-10. Revealing Answers in a Commit-Reveal Puzzle

```
function reveal(uint answer) public {
    require(block.number > guessDeadline);
    require(block.number < revealDeadline);
    require(createCommitment(msg.sender, answer) ==
            commitments[msg.sender]);
    require(createCommitment(creator, answer) ==
            commitments[creator]);
    require(!isWinner(msg.sender));

    winners.push(msg.sender);
}
```

The function can be called only after the guessing deadline and before the revealing deadline. The answer must match both the player's guessing submission and the creator's answer submission. This requires creating two commitments, one using the player's address and one using the creator's address. If both commitments match, and the player is not already in the list of winners, we add the player to the list of winners.

To check whether a player is in the winners list, we will create a separate function, isWinner (Listing 9-11), because the code will need to be reused later, when claiming the prize.

Listing 9-11. Checking Whether an Address Is in the List of Winners

```
function isWinner (address user) public view returns (bool) {
    bool winner = false;
    for (uint i=0; i < winners.length; i++) {
        if (winners[i] == user) {
            winner = true;
            break;
        }
    }
    return winner;
}
```

This function loops through the list of winners, checking whether any of them are the provided address. If one is, the loop breaks and the function returns `true`. If not, the function returns `false`.

Any player who makes the list of winners can claim their prize after the reveal deadline is over (Listing 9-12).

Listing 9-12. Claiming a Commit-Reveal Puzzle Prize

```
function claim () public {
    require(block.number > revealDeadline);
    require(claimed[msg.sender] == false);
    require(isWinner(msg.sender));

    uint payout = totalPrize / winners.length;
    claimed[msg.sender] = true;
    msg.sender.transfer(payout);
}
```

Prizes can be claimed anytime after the reveal deadline. The total prize is split among all the winners. The function marks the player as having claimed their reward so that they cannot double-claim their prize.

Deploying this contract requires the same steps as deploying the simple prize contract. Deploy the contract with a fake commitment first, use the dummy contract to generate the answer commitment, and then deploy the real contract with the answer commitment. The code can be found in `migrations/14_commit_reveal_puzzle.js` in the GitHub repo. There is nothing new from the simple prize migration, so it is not reproduced here.

Additional Prize Challenges

In Exercises 9-2 and 9-3, we present two additional challenges that will allow you to interact directly with the mainnet. In the first challenge, we provide a prize puzzle for you to solve; and in the second one, we ask you to create your own.

EXERCISE 9-2. FIRST TO THE PRIZE

We have deployed a simple prize puzzle to the Ethereum mainnet. The Etherscan page for the contract is at `https://etherscan.io/address/0x73388dc2f89777cbdf53e5352f516cd703d070a6`. The answer to the following question will unlock the 0.02 ether prize:

`What is the sum of the first 1 million primes?`

EXERCISE 9-3. CREATE YOUR OWN PUZZLE

Now that you've seen a series of example prize puzzles, it's time to create your own. Deploy a prize puzzle with your answer commitment, and then head over to the GitHub issue created for this exercise (`https://github.com/k26dr/ethereum-games/issues/2`). Reply to the issue with your question and a link to the Etherscan page for the contract. If you can't or don't want to create your own puzzle, donate to one of the existing ones.

Summary

In this chapter, we reviewed two types of prize puzzles: one that unlocks a prize immediately upon receiving a correct guess, and another that uses a commit-reveal method and allows multiple winners. We walked extensively through the logic behind answer obfuscation, which is necessary for running a fair contest.

In the next chapter, we cover prediction markets, which allow us to bet on the probability of future events.

CHAPTER 10

Prediction Markets

On the gambling spectrum, *prediction markets* are somewhere between proposition bets ("prop" bets) and stock markets. They don't enjoy the full legitimacy of stock markets, but they tend to be less silly and address more serious matters than your standard prop bet. Prediction markets start by posing a yes/no question about a future event with a verifiable answer. Users can then bet on the possibility of the event by buying or selling shares in the market.

Here is an example of a typical prediction market question:

```
Will Ethereum trade at $2,000 or higher on GDAX on January 1,
2019 00:00.000 UTC?
```

This is a clear question with a publicly verifiable answer ending at an exact time. Good prediction market questions eliminate all sources of ambiguity so that users can verify and track the state of their bet.

The format of this chapter is slightly different from previous chapters. Instead of presenting multiple contracts, we spend the majority of the chapter walking through a complex prediction market contract. At the end, we cover resolution methods that you will be free to implement on your own.

© Kedar Iyer and Chris Dannen 2018
K. Iyer and C. Dannen, *Building Games with Ethereum Smart Contracts*,
https://doi.org/10.1007/978-1-4842-3492-1_10

Contract Overview

In a prediction market, trading is split into shares. Each share pays out 100 wei if the answer resolves to Yes, and 0 wei if the answer resolves to No. In this way, the price per share reflects the market's possibility of resolving to Yes. If the price for the preceding market is 60, the market thinks there's a 60% probability that Ethereum will be above $2,000 at the beginning of 2019.

To start a market, a market creator must post collateral for the payouts, 100 wei for each share. If the market resolves to Yes, the collateral is paid out to the owners of the shares. If the market resolves to No, the collateral is paid back to the market creator. In exchange for taking on this risk, the market creator is allowed to charge a fee on every trade. Typical fees on cryptocurrency exchanges are between 0.1% and 0.25%. Our contract will charge 0.2% on each side of a trade, but this can be changed easily.

The full contract is presented in Listing 10-1, with commentary and analysis to follow.

Listing 10-1. Prediction Market

```
contract PredictionMarket {
    enum OrderType { Buy, Sell }
    enum Result { Open, Yes, No }

    struct Order {
        address user;
        OrderType orderType;
        uint amount;
        uint price;
    }
```

```
uint public constant TX_FEE_NUMERATOR = 1;
uint public constant TX_FEE_DENOMINATOR = 500;

address public owner;
Result public result;
uint public deadline;
uint public counter;
uint public collateral;
mapping(uint => Order) public orders;
mapping(address => uint) public shares;
mapping(address => uint) public balances;

event OrderPlaced(uint orderId, address user, OrderType
orderType, uint amount, uint price);
event TradeMatched(uint orderId, address user, uint amount);
event OrderCanceled(uint orderId);
event Payout(address user, uint amount);

function PredictionMarket (uint duration) public payable {
    require(msg.value > 0);

    owner = msg.sender;
    deadline = now + duration;
    shares[msg.sender] = msg.value / 100;
    collateral = msg.value;
}

function orderBuy (uint price) public payable {
    require(now < deadline);
    require(msg.value > 0);
    require(price >= 0);
    require(price <= 100);
    uint amount = msg.value / price;
```

```
        counter++;
        orders[counter] = Order(msg.sender, OrderType.Buy,
        amount, price);
        OrderPlaced(counter, msg.sender, OrderType.Buy, amount,
        price);
    }

    function orderSell (uint price, uint amount) public {
        require(now < deadline);
        require(shares[msg.sender] >= amount);
        require(price >= 0);
        require(price <= 100);

        shares[msg.sender] -= amount;

        counter++;
        orders[counter] = Order(msg.sender, OrderType.Sell, amount,
                                price);
        OrderPlaced(counter, msg.sender, OrderType.Sell,
        amount, price);
    }

    function tradeBuy (uint orderId) public payable {
        Order storage order = orders[orderId];

        require(now < deadline);
        require(order.user != msg.sender);
        require(order.orderType == OrderType.Sell);
        require(order.amount > 0);
        require(msg.value > 0);
        require(msg.value <= order.amount * order.price);

        uint amount = msg.value / order.price;
        uint fee = (amount * order.price) * TX_FEE_NUMERATOR /
                                            TX_FEE_DENOMINATOR;
```

```
    uint feeShares = amount * TX_FEE_NUMERATOR / TX_FEE_
    DENOMINATOR;

    shares[msg.sender] += (amount - feeShares);
    shares[owner] += feeShares;

    balances[order.user] += (amount * order.price) - fee;
    balances[owner] += fee;

    order.amount -= amount;
    if (order.amount == 0)
        delete orders[orderId];

    TradeMatched(orderId, msg.sender, amount);
}
function tradeSell (uint orderId, uint amount) public {
    Order storage order = orders[orderId];

    require(now < deadline);
    require(order.user != msg.sender);
    require(order.orderType == OrderType.Buy);
    require(order.amount > 0);
    require(amount <= order.amount);
    require(shares[msg.sender] >= amount);

    uint fee = (amount * order.price) * TX_FEE_NUMERATOR /
                            TX_FEE_DENOMINATOR;
    uint feeShares = amount * TX_FEE_NUMERATOR /
                            TX_FEE_DENOMINATOR;

    shares[msg.sender] -= amount;
    shares[order.user] += (amount - feeShares);
    shares[owner] += feeShares;
```

```
        balances[msg.sender] += (amount * order.price) - fee;
        balances[owner] += fee;

        order.amount -= amount;
        if (order.amount == 0)
            delete orders[orderId];

        TradeMatched(orderId, msg.sender, amount);
    }

    function cancelOrder (uint orderId) public {
        Order storage order = orders[orderId];

        require(order.user == msg.sender);

        if (order.orderType == OrderType.Buy)
            balances[msg.sender] += order.amount * order.price;
        else
            shares[msg.sender] += order.amount;

        delete orders[orderId];
        OrderCanceled(orderId);
    }

    function resolve (bool _result) public {
        require(now > deadline);
        require(msg.sender == owner);
        require(result == Result.Open);

        result = _result ? Result.Yes : Result.No;
        if (result == Result.No)
            balances[owner] += collateral;
    }
```

```
function withdraw () public {
    uint payout = balances[msg.sender];
    balances[msg.sender] = 0;

    if (result == Result.Yes) {
        payout += shares[msg.sender] * 100;
        shares[msg.sender] = 0;
    }

    msg.sender.transfer(payout);
    Payout(msg.sender, payout);
    }

}
```

The contract defines three custom data types:

- OrderType: An enum, the type of an order—Buy or Sell.

- Result: An enum representing the current resolution of the market. Open means the market is actively trading or has not been resolved. Yes or No refer to resolved markets. A Yes result pays out shareholders, whereas a No result returns the collateral to the market creator.

- Order: A struct representing an active order on the market. It contains information on the user who placed the order, the type of order (Buy or Sell), the amount of outstanding shares in the order, and the price of the order.

The contract contains the following constants and state variables:

- TX_FEE_NUMERATOR: The transaction fee is set at .002 (0.2%), but because Solidity doesn't support decimals, it needs to be defined as a fraction in two parts. The exact fraction is 1/500. This constant is the numerator of that fraction.

- TX_FEE_DENOMINATOR: The denominator portion of the 1/500 transaction fee.

- owner: The creator of the contract or market creator.

- result: The current state of the contract result—Open, Yes, or No.

- deadline: A UNIX timestamp corresponding to the end of permitted market trading.

- counter: An incrementing integer used to assign order IDs.

- collateral: The value of the collateral held in the contract in wei.

- orders: The order book. A mapping from order IDs to Order structs.

- shares: A mapping from user addresses to the number of shares held by the user.

- balances: A standard mapping from user addresses to internal balances in wei.

The contract constructor is payable and sets the number of shares in the market (Listing 10-2). It takes a duration as its only argument and uses it to set the deadline.

Listing 10-2. Prediction Market Constructor

```
function PredictionMarket (uint duration) public payable {
    require(msg.value > 0);

    owner = msg.sender;
    deadline =  now + duration;
    shares[msg.sender] = msg.value / 100;
    collateral = msg.value;
}
```

The full collateral for each share's payout must be posted upon contract creation. Because each share has a potential payout of 100 wei, the number of shares created is the amount of wei sent divided by 100. The collateral will be returned to the creator if the market resolves to No.

Tracking State with Events

Most large Solidity contracts cannot expose their full internal state with just getter functions. This makes building a user-friendly front end nearly impossible without additional information. For instance, a front end that wishes to display a full order book would not be able to retrieve this information from our contract because it is impossible to determine the set keys for a `mapping` from a contract.

Events and logs fill in this gap by providing an easily parsable history of all actions that have occurred in the contract. They are stored in a separate data structure from the contract state so they are accessible by only front ends and clients (see "Logging and Events" in Chapter 4). By recording every relevant action in the contract, a front end can reconstruct the full state of the contract.

Our prediction market contains four events. Combined with the public state variables, they can be used to construct a full snapshot of the contract state to display to users. The four events are as follows:

- `OrderPlaced`: Logged when an order is added to the order book. Contains information about the `price`, `amount`, `user`, and `orderType` (`Buy` or `Sell`) of the order. This event alone is not sufficient to capture the full state of the order book because it does not cover canceled or matched orders.

- `TradeMatched`: Logged when an order is matched and a trade is executed. References the `orderId` of the matched order, the `amount` of shares traded, and the `user` who matched the order. Orders can be partially filled, so matching less than the full `amount` of an order will leave it on the order book.

- `OrderCanceled`: Logged when an order is canceled. A canceled order is deleted from the order book. An order can be partially filled when canceled, so a single order could have all three `OrderPlaced`, `TradeMatched`, and `OrderCanceled` events.

- `Payout`: Logged when a user makes a withdrawal. Logs the `amount` in wei of the payout along with the `user` address.

Trading Shares

A user can take five types of trading actions in our prediction market: place a buy order, place a sell order, fill a buy order, fill a sell order, and cancel an open order. Each of these actions has a corresponding public function in our smart contract.

Listing 10-3 contains code for placing a buy order.

Listing 10-3. Placing a Buy Order

```
function orderBuy (uint price) public payable {
    require(now < deadline);
    require(msg.value > 0);
    require(price >= 0);
    require(price <= 100);
    uint amount = msg.value / price;
```

```
counter++;
orders[counter] = Order(msg.sender, OrderType.Buy,
                        amount, price);
OrderPlaced(counter, msg.sender, OrderType.Buy, amount,
            price);
}
```

A buy order must be placed at a specified price between 0 and 100 inclusive. All orders must be placed before the market deadline. The amount of shares in the order is calculated automatically from the ether value sent with the order and the price. Sending an order with no ether value will throw an error.

The counter is incremented to generate a fresh order ID, and then the order is created and stored in the order book. An event is logged to indicate that a new order has been added to the book.

One small nuance is hidden from view here: Solidity creates structs in memory, not storage. When Solidity encounters a memory struct being saved to a state variable as in the preceding code, it automatically converts the memory struct to a storage struct before updating the state tree. The same automatic conversion does not occur for local variables. If you attempt to store the created struct to an Order storage instead of an Order memory variable, it will throw an error.

Listing 10-4 contains code for placing a sell order.

Listing 10-4. Placing a Sell Order

```
function orderSell (uint price, uint amount) public {
    require(now < deadline);
    require(shares[msg.sender] >= amount);
    require(price >= 0);
    require(price <= 100);

    shares[msg.sender] -= amount;
```

```
    counter++;
    orders[counter] = Order(msg.sender, OrderType.Sell,
                            amount, price);
    OrderPlaced(counter, msg.sender, OrderType.Sell,
                amount, price);
}
```

Placing a sell order is similar to placing a buy order. The order must be placed before the deadline, and the price must be from 0–100. The user must specify a number of shares to sell no greater than the number of shares they currently hold.

When a sell order is placed, the number of shares in the order is deducted from the user's share holdings. This is done to prevent users from double-listing their shares.

Listing 10-5 contains code for filling a buy order. It is called `tradeSell` because the act of filling a buy order requires a user to sell their shares.

Listing 10-5. Filling a Buy Order

```
function tradeSell (uint orderId, uint amount) public {
    Order storage order = orders[orderId];

    require(now < deadline);
    require(order.user != msg.sender);
    require(order.orderType == OrderType.Buy);
    require(order.amount > 0);
    require(amount <= order.amount);
    require(shares[msg.sender] >= amount);

    uint fee = (amount * order.price) * TX_FEE_NUMERATOR /
                                       TX_FEE_DENOMINATOR;
    uint feeShares = amount * TX_FEE_NUMERATOR /
                             TX_FEE_DENOMINATOR;
```

```
    shares[msg.sender] -= amount;
    shares[order.user] += (amount - feeShares);
    shares[owner] += feeShares;

    balances[msg.sender] += (amount * order.price) - fee;
    balances[owner] += fee;

    order.amount -= amount;
    if (order.amount == 0)
        delete orders[orderId];

    TradeMatched(orderId, msg.sender, amount);
}
```

The order-filling functions are quite complex. A buy order is filled by specifying an order ID and an amount of shares that must be less than or equal to both the number of shares in the order and the number of shares held by the user.

A user cannot fill their own buy order. This is a practice known as *wash trading*, which is prohibited by most exchanges because it creates artificial volume.

When an order is filled, the contract takes a fee from each side of the trade and gives it to the market creator. The buyer is receiving shares, and the seller is receiving ether, so the fee for the buyer is taken in shares, and the fee for the seller is taken in ether.

When updating the shares, the sale amount of shares is deducted from the seller and added to the buyer minus the fee. When updating the balances, ether is added to the seller minus the fee, but the balance is not subtracted from the buyer because the buyer is sending their funds directly to the function.

Solidity doesn't permit decimal arithmetic, so a fractional fee is calculated by using TX_FEE_NUMERATOR and TX_FEE_DENOMINATOR. Because the fee is 1/500 and only integer fees are permitted, the fee calculation will not be entirely accurate, and small trades of less than 500 wei can be placed without incurring a fee. This number is so much smaller than the gas fee for a transaction, however, that it is not a major security flaw.

Orders can partially fill, so the amount of shares filled by the seller is subtracted from the number of open shares in the order. If an order is completely filled and has no open shares remaining, it is deleted from the order book.

After all of the trade logic is complete, an event is logged with the details of the trade.

Listing 10-6 contains code for filling a sell order. It is called tradeBuy because filling a sell order requires a user to buy shares.

Listing 10-6. Filling a Sell Order

```
function tradeBuy (uint orderId) public payable {
    Order storage order = orders[orderId];

    require(now < deadline);
    require(order.user != msg.sender);
    require(order.orderType == OrderType.Sell);
    require(order.amount > 0);
    require(msg.value > 0);
    require(msg.value <= order.amount * order.price);

    uint amount = msg.value / order.price;
    uint fee = (amount * order.price) * TX_FEE_NUMERATOR /
                                        TX_FEE_DENOMINATOR;
    uint feeShares = amount * TX_FEE_NUMERATOR /
                             TX_FEE_DENOMINATOR;

    shares[msg.sender] += (amount - feeShares);
    shares[owner] += feeShares;
```

```
    balances[order.user] += (amount * order.price) - fee;
    balances[owner] += fee;

    order.amount -= amount;
    if (order.amount == 0)
        delete orders[orderId];

    TradeMatched(orderId, msg.sender, amount);
}
```

Filling a sell order is similar to filling a buy order. Instead of including an amount with the transaction, the buyer sends ether with the transaction, and the amount of shares to buy is automatically calculated. The transfers and fees are calculated and distributed the same as before, except this time the shares are not subtracted from the seller because the subtraction took place when the sell order was placed.

Listing 10-7 contains code for canceling an order.

Listing 10-7. Canceling an Order

```
function cancelOrder (uint orderId) public {
    Order storage order = orders[orderId];

    require(order.user == msg.sender);

    if (order.orderType == OrderType.Buy)
        balances[msg.sender] += order.amount * order.price;
    else
        shares[msg.sender] += order.amount;

    delete orders[orderId];
    OrderCanceled(orderId);
}
```

The function is called by specifying the ID of the order to cancel. Only the user who placed the order can cancel it. For buy orders, the ether value of the remaining shares is refunded to the user's balance. For sell orders, the remaining shares are credited back to the user's holdings. The order is then deleted, and an event is logged specifying the ID of the deleted order.

Resolving Markets

Resolving prediction markets on blockchains is still an open area of research. Our contract uses simple single-oracle resolution. Other systems include multiple-oracle resolution and Schelling point consensus. We will discuss the last two in theory, but leave the coding of the them to you as an exercise.

Single Oracle

An *oracle* is a user or program on a blockchain network that brings external off-chain information onto the chain. Because Ethereum can't interact directly with the HTTP Web or other blockchain networks, oracles are required to bring any external information on-chain. A single-oracle system is the simplest form of oracle. A single user is given exclusive permission to upload the result of the market to the contract. The code is given in Listing 10-8.

Listing 10-8. Single-Oracle Resolution

```
function resolve (bool _result) public {
    require(now > deadline);
    require(msg.sender == owner);
    require(result == Result.Open);
```

```
    result = _result ? Result.Yes : Result.No;
    if (result == Result.No)
        balances[owner] += collateral;
}
```

Anytime after the deadline, if the result is still open, the owner (and only the owner) can set the result of the market. The function takes a boolean as its single argument. If true, the market resolves to Yes. If false, the market resolves to No. If the market resolves to No, the collateral is paid out to the owner. If the market resolves to Yes, users can claim their payouts by using the code in Listing 10-9.

Listing 10-9. Claiming Payouts

```
function withdraw () public {
    uint payout = balances[msg.sender];
    balances[msg.sender] = 0;

    if (result == Result.Yes) {
        payout += shares[msg.sender] * 100;
        shares[msg.sender] = 0;
    }

    msg.sender.transfer(payout);
    Payout(msg.sender, payout);
}
```

The payout total has only two parts. Refunds from canceled orders and ether from share sales are already recorded in the internal balances. Share payouts must be computed separately, 100 wei for every share held if the market has resolved to Yes. These are combined, paid out to the user, and both the balances and the shares are zeroed out. An event is logged to signal the front end that a payout has processed.

Fees and collateral can be claimed by the owner through this function as well. Fees in both ether and shares are credited to the owner's balance and share holdings during the contract, while collateral is credited to the owner's balance.

Multiple Oracle

Single-oracle resolution systems have a number of flaws. An error in resolution is irreversible, so a slip of mind can lead to the market being resolved incorrectly. Additionally, the oracle may have a stake in the market through other unknown addresses and resolve the game to their own benefit instead of correctly. The pseudonymity of Ethereum addresses would make it hard to trace the cheater.

Multiple-oracle resolution offers a slight advantage over single-oracle resolution. Instead of having a single oracle determine the result, multiple oracles would have to verify the result before the market resolves.

One way of implementing this is with N of M verification, where two-of-three or four-of-five oracles must agree on a result for a game to be resolved properly. A five-oracle system with four or five oracles required for resolution is a good standard.

For a publicly verifiable event, there should be no doubt as to which way the market should resolve. The purpose of using multiple oracles is to prevent human error and cheating, not clear up an ambiguous result. Allowing for one dissenting oracle is enough to account for human error or a lone cheater. Anything more than that is likely a sign of active collusion. For a market that does not clear the threshold for resolving in either direction, the best practice is to nullify the market and return everybody's initial investments.

In Exercise 10-1, we will implement this multi-oracle system.

EXERCISE 10-1. MULTIPLE ORACLES

Modify the resolution system in our PredictionMarket contract so that four out of five oracles must agree on the result for a market to resolve. Implementing refunds for unresolvable markets is a much more complex task and can be left out for now.

Schelling Point Consensus

Schelling points are a generalization of the multiple-oracle system. Instead of a fixed number of predetermined oracles, anybody is free to participate in Schelling point resolution. Game theory research sometimes refers to Schelling points as *focal points*.

To participate in a prediction market Schelling point, every user stakes a nontrivial amount of ether on their proposed resolution of the market, Yes or No. At the end of the staking period, the market resolves to the side with the most votes. All the ether goes into a staking pool that gets split by the winners of the vote. If a market resolves to Yes and you vote No, you lose your stake and it gets split by all voters who voted Yes.

This provides a powerful incentive for people to vote with the side that they think will be the winner. If the voting system is large and decentralized enough, collusion becomes difficult, and users gravitate to a focal point that they believe others will gravitate to as well. In this case, the focal point is the correct resolution for the market, so in theory everyone voting in their own interest should vote for the correct resolution.

This system has a couple of apparent flaws. The largest is the possibility for a highly invested market participant to game the system by submitting a bunch of votes under different addresses. There is no way to prevent a user from generating and staking with multiple addresses in Ethereum without additional restrictions on who can vote. Attacks on blockchains that use multiple addresses like this are called *Sybil attacks*.

To prevent Sybil attacks, one possible restriction is to allow only market participants holding shares at the end of the market to vote. Unfortunately, all users are incentivized to vote Yes so that they can receive a payout, so collusion becomes a major issue there as well.

Schelling point resolution in blockchain systems is mostly theoretical at this point and hasn't been extensively tested. Augur, a decentralized prediction market creator, has proposed using Schelling points to resolve its markets with restrictions on who can vote in the Schelling points determined using an internal token (REP). This should give us data about the real-world effectiveness of Schelling points on Ethereum in the near future.

Summary

Prediction markets allow users to bet on and profit from the probability of an arbitrary event occurring. Using our smart contract, users can buy or sell shares in a prediction market, where each share pays out 100 wei if the market resolves to Yes.

Every order, trade, and payout logs an event to the Ethereum log database. These logs allow front ends to determine the full state of a contract and present an order book to users, something they would be unable to do with just the getter functions built into Solidity.

Our contract used single-oracle resolution to determine the result of the market. It is simple, but also susceptible to human error and cheating. Multiple-oracle resolution reduces the likelihood of a market resolving incorrectly. The most generalized version of multiple-oracle resolution is Schelling point consensus. Schelling point consensus looks promising, but it has yet to be implemented successfully in a real-world contract.

In the next and final chapter, we will dive straight into our gambling roots and cover casino games.

CHAPTER 11

Gambling

Online casinos and gambling sites are notorious for rigging their games. Blockchain-based gambling games offer users a chance to play games with provably fair odds and minimal or no house fees. In this chapter, we cover two gambling games: Satoshi dice and roulette.

Gameplay Limitations

Casino games aren't a perfect fit for blockchains. The problem lies in random-number generation. Secure RNG requires two transactions spaced at least a minute or so apart, making anything more than single-play games nearly impossible on-chain. A multiturn game such as blackjack or poker would be painstakingly slow and practically unusable using completely on-chain implementations. A hybrid approach in which portions of the game are run off-chain and then results are committed to the chain would be required to run these games. Because off-chain games are not the focus of this book, we stick to single-turn games in this chapter.

Satoshi Dice

Satoshi dice was an early Bitcoin gambling game that was the first widely used application on a blockchain. For a while, it was responsible for half the transactions on the Bitcoin network. The company ran into legal problems after a while, but the idea has lived on, and many alternate implementations of it still exist today.

© Kedar Iyer and Chris Dannen 2018
K. Iyer and C. Dannen, *Building Games with Ethereum Smart Contracts*,
https://doi.org/10.1007/978-1-4842-3492-1_11

The idea behind the game is simple. Along with your Bitcoin transaction, submit a number from 0–65,535 (2^{16} = 65,536). The game then generates a random number in the same range by using a secret seed. If the generated number is below the submitted number, the user wins money. The amount of money won is dependent on the submitted number. The lower the number, the higher the multiplier and payout (32,000 = ~2x, 16,000 = ~4x).

To provide provably fair gameplay, the original Satoshi dice published the hash of its secret seed to the blockchain along with the betting address. They would then periodically publish old seeds so that old bets could be verified.

We want to convert this game into a decentralized, trustless setup. Under the old system, the onus was on the user to verify each of their own bets to make sure no cheating was occurring. Under our system, there will be no way for a nonminer to cheat, and even miners will be able to only minimally influence outcomes.

Listing 11-1 gives the code for our implementation before discussing it in detail.

Listing 11-1. Satoshi Dice

```
contract SatoshiDice {
    struct Bet {
        address user;
        uint block;
        uint cap;
        uint amount;
    }

    uint public constant FEE_NUMERATOR = 1;
    uint public constant FEE_DENOMINATOR = 100;
    uint public constant MAXIMUM_CAP = 100000;
    uint public constant MAXIMUM_BET_SIZE = 1e18;
```

```
address owner;
uint public counter = 0;
mapping(uint => Bet) public bets;

event BetPlaced(uint id, address user, uint cap, uint amount);
event Roll(uint id, uint rolled);

function SatoshiDice () public {
    owner = msg.sender;
}

function wager (uint cap) public payable {
    require(cap <= MAXIMUM_CAP);
    require(msg.value <= MAXIMUM_BET_SIZE);
    counter++;
    bets[counter] = Bet(msg.sender, block.number + 3, cap,
    msg.value);
    BetPlaced(counter, msg.sender, cap, msg.value);
}

function roll(uint id) public {
    Bet storage bet = bets[id];
    require(msg.sender == bet.user);
    require(block.number >= bet.block);
    require(block.number <= bet.block + 255);

    bytes32 random = keccak256(block.blockhash(bet.block), id);
    uint rolled = uint(random) % MAXIMUM_CAP;
    if (rolled < bet.cap) {
        uint payout = bet.amount * MAXIMUM_CAP / bet.cap;
        uint fee = payout * FEE_NUMERATOR / FEE_DENOMINATOR;
        payout -= fee;
        msg.sender.transfer(payout);
    }
```

```
        Roll(id, rolled);
        delete bets[id];
    }

    function fund () payable public {}

    function kill () public {
        require(msg.sender == owner);
        selfdestruct(owner);
    }
}
```

The contract defines a custom Bet struct containing information about the bet. It contains the user address, the block number from which the blockhash will be pulled, the number submitted with the bet (cap), and the amount of the bet.

The contract has four constants:

- FEE_NUMERATOR: The numerator portion of the fee. The fee is set to 1%.

- FEE_DENOMINATOR: The denominator portion of the fee.

- MAXIMUM_CAP: The maximum value of the number that can be submitted with a bet. In the original Satoshi dice, this was 2^{16} so it could fit in 2 bytes. Because we have access to integer types, we will set this to a more pleasant number: 100,000 (10^5).

- MAXIMUM_BET_SIZE: The maximum value that can be wagered in a single bet. This is mostly to prevent user error from accidentally wagering too much money. It does *not* provide a guarantee that a winning bet can be paid out. It is up to the user to verify that the contract contains enough money to pay off their bet before placing it. If the contract cannot, the user will have to wait until the contract accumulates enough ether to make the payout. The inclusion of the fee ensures that the contract balance will slowly increase.

The majority of the state complexity is in the Bet struct, so there are only three state variables:

- owner: The creator of the contract. Only used for killing the contract; the owner has no other special rights.

- counter: An incrementing counter used to assign unique IDs.

- bets: A mapping from bet IDs to Bet structs.

There are two events as well for front-ends to consume: a BetPlaced event for when a wager is placed, and a Roll event for when the wager is resolved.

The contract has two primary functions: one for placing the wager and locking in the block number for the RNG, and one for resolving the bet by generating a random number. The wager function is reproduced in Listing 11-2.

Listing 11-2. Wagering on Satoshi Dice

```
function wager (uint cap) public payable {
    require(cap <= MAXIMUM_CAP);
    require(msg.value <= MAXIMUM_BET_SIZE);

    counter++;
    bets[counter] = Bet(msg.sender, block.number + 3, cap,
                        msg.value);
    BetPlaced(counter, msg.sender, cap, msg.value);
}
```

The wager takes a cap as an argument and accepts ether for the bet. The cap must be below the MAXIMUM_CAP, and the ether value must be below the MAXIMUM_BET_SIZE. The counter is incremented to generate a new ID and then a new Bet is saved to the state. The block number for the RNG is set three blocks in the future, a sufficient amount forward that the blockhash is unknown.

The second major function is the roll function (Listing 11-3). This function "rolls" the dice and resolves the wager by using the blockhash from the block specified in the wager.

Listing 11-3. Resolving Satoshi Dice Wagers

```
function roll(uint id) public {
    Bet storage bet = bets[id];
    require(msg.sender == bet.user);
    require(block.number >= bet.block);
    require(block.number <= bet.block + 255);

    bytes32 random = keccak256(block.blockhash(bet.block),
                               id);
    uint rolled = uint(random) % MAXIMUM_CAP;
    if (rolled < bet.cap) {
        uint payout = bet.amount * MAXIMUM_CAP / bet.cap;
        uint fee = payout * FEE_NUMERATOR /
                            FEE_DENOMINATOR;
        payout -= fee;
        msg.sender.transfer(payout);
    }

    Roll(id, rolled);
    delete bets[id];
}
```

A bet ID must be included with the function call so that the function knows which bet to resolve. Only the user who originated the bet can "roll" the dice for the bet, and that user must wait three blocks after wagering to do so. The user must trigger the roll within 255 blocks of the bet block or forfeit their wager. This is because Solidity stores only the 256 most recent blockhashes, and waiting longer than that will lead to a deterministic roll in which the blockhash is always 0x0.

A pseudorandom number is generated using the blockhash of the specified block and the bet ID. Because the bet ID is unique to each bet, no two bets will generate the same pseudorandom number. The random bytes generated are converted into a "dice roll" in the acceptable range. If the rolled number is less than the bet cap, the user receives a payout.

To calculate the payout, the bet amount is multiplied by the ratio of the maximum cap to the bet cap. The maximum cap is fixed, so the lower the bet cap, the higher the multiplier. To allow the contract to gradually accept larger and larger bets, a 1% fee is taken from each bet. The fee is retained by the contract, and the remainder of the payout is sent to the user.

After the bet has been resolved, the bet is deleted. This prevents the bet from being double-claimed by the user and cleans up unneeded data from the blockchain. A deleted struct sets each of its members to the zero value for the data type. The user of a deleted bet will be the zero address, so it will throw an error when the function attempts to verify that msg.sender is the bet user.

Two additional simple functions are included in the contract. A standard kill function is included to allow the owner to self-destruct the contract and claim fees. A payable function to fund the contract is included as well. Before fees start accumulating, the contract will have to be funded with enough ether to allow initial bets to pay out.

If you would like to play Satoshi dice on the mainnet, you will be able to do so in Exercise 11-1.

EXERCISE 11-1. ROLL YOUR DICE

We have deployed a version of our Satoshi dice contract to the Ethereum mainnet. The Etherscan page for the contract is at `https://etherscan.io/address/0x55283a2f07be1b95e1e417af7efaab6750fedd0d`. Play the game, try to hack the contract—whatever you'd like. The ether from the fees will accumulate in the contract, and if anybody successfully hacks the contract, the ether is theirs. We will not come after you.

Roulette

Roulette is a classic casino game that translates well to a blockchain implementation. The game traditionally has a wagering phase and a spinning phase in which wagers are resolved. We have re-created that setup with our contract.

Before the spin, users can wager on either a Color bet or a Number bet. Traditionally, roulette tables permit a wider variety of bets such as High/Low, Odd/Even, Split, and more, but we have left the implementation of those additional bet varieties as an exercise for you.

Listing 11-4 contains the full roulette contract. Because we have an existing contract called Roulette from Chapter 5, we have named this one CasinoRoulette to prevent conflicts.

Listing 11-4. Roulette Contract

```
contract CasinoRoulette {
    enum BetType { Color, Number }

    struct Bet {
        address user;
        uint amount;
```

```
    BetType betType;
    uint block;

    // @prop choice: interpretation is based on BetType
        // BetType.Color: 0=black, 1=red
        // BetType.Number: -1=00, 0-36 for individual numbers
    int choice;
}

uint public constant NUM_POCKETS = 38;
// RED_NUMBERS and BLACK_NUMBERS are constant, but
// Solidity doesn't support array constants yet so
// we use storage arrays instead
uint8[18] public RED_NUMBERS = [
    1, 3, 5, 7, 9, 12,
    14, 16, 18, 19, 21, 23,
    25, 27, 30, 32, 34, 36
];
uint8[18] public BLACK_NUMBERS = [
    2, 4, 6, 8, 10, 11,
    13, 15, 17, 20, 22, 24,
    26, 28, 29, 31, 33, 35
];
// maps wheel numbers to colors
mapping(int => int) public COLORS;

address public owner;
uint public counter = 0;
mapping(uint => Bet) public bets;

event BetPlaced(address user, uint amount, BetType betType,
uint block, int choice);
event Spin(uint id, int landed);
```

```
function CasinoRoulette () public {
    owner = msg.sender;
    for (uint i=0; i < 18; i++) {
        COLORS[RED_NUMBERS[i]] = 1;
    }
}

function wager (BetType betType, int choice) payable public {
    require(msg.value > 0);
    if (betType == BetType.Color)
        require(choice == 0 || choice == 1);
    else
        require(choice >= -1 && choice <= 36);
    counter++;
    bets[counter] = Bet(msg.sender, msg.value, betType,
                        block.number + 3, choice);
    BetPlaced(msg.sender, msg.value, betType, block.number + 3,
            choice);
}

function spin (uint id) public {
    Bet storage bet = bets[id];
    require(msg.sender == bet.user);
    require(block.number >= bet.block);
    require(block.number <= bet.block + 255);
    bytes32 random = keccak256(block.blockhash(bet.block), id);
    int landed = int(uint(random) % NUM_POCKETS) - 1;
```

```
        if (bet.betType == BetType.Color) {
            if (landed > 0 && COLORS[landed] == bet.choice)
                msg.sender.transfer(bet.amount * 2);
        }
        else if (bet.betType == BetType.Number) {
            if (landed == bet.choice)
                msg.sender.transfer(bet.amount * 35);
        }

        delete bets[id];
        Spin(id, landed);
    }

    function fund () public payable {}

    function kill () public {
        require(msg.sender == owner);
        selfdestruct(owner);
    }
}
```

Like Satoshi dice, the roulette contains a Bet struct as well. It tracks
the user, amount, and block just like Satoshi dice, but also includes two
additional fields, betType and choice. betType is an enum defined at the
top of the contract. It currently has only two accepted values, Color and
Number. A winning Color bet pays out 2×, and a winning Number bet pays
out 35×. You will be responsible for adding more bet types in the exercise
at the end of this section.

The choice property has different allowed values for each betType.
For BetType.Color, choice must be either 0 for block, or 1 for red. For
BetType.Number, it can be –1 for double-zero (00), or 0–36 for the numbers
0–36 on a roulette wheel.

The contract contains one constant, and three pseudoconstants that do not change in value:

- NUM_POCKETS: The number of pockets in a roulette wheel, 38.

- RED_NUMBERS: The numbers that correspond to red-colored pockets on a roulette wheel. Solidity doesn't support array constants, so this is held in a public nonconstant field instead.

- BLACK_NUMBERS: The numbers that correspond to black-colored pockets on a roulette wheel.

- COLORS: A mapping that maps from roulette wheel numbers to colors. The permitted values are 0 for black, and 1 for red. This mapping doesn't hold any new information, but it makes executing the color-checking logic much simpler.

The contract has three state variables and two events. They are the exact same as the state variables and events in Satoshi dice, so we do not go over them again here. The only small difference to note is that the Roll event from Satoshi dice has been renamed Spin here.

The constructor function reproduced in Listing 11-5 populates the COLORS pseudoconstant.

Listing 11-5. CasinoRoulette Constructor

```
function CasinoRoulette () public {
    owner = msg.sender;
    for (uint i=0; i < 18; i++) {
        COLORS[RED_NUMBERS[i]] = 1;
    }
}
```

The COLORS pseudoconstant is populated by looping through the list of red numbers and setting all their values to 1. This will be useful later for determining the color of a number in the spin logic.

The first of the two major functions is the wager function in Listing 11-6.

Listing 11-6. Wagering on Roulette

```
function wager (BetType betType, int choice) payable public {
    require(msg.value > 0);
    if (betType == BetType.Color)
        require(choice == 0 || choice == 1);
    else
        require(choice >= -1 && choice <= 36);
    counter++;
    bets[counter] = Bet(msg.sender, msg.value, betType,
                        block.number + 3, choice);
    BetPlaced(msg.sender, msg.value, betType,
              block.number + 3, choice);
}
```

Wagers are placed by specifying a bet type and choice. Wager transactions must include a nonzero ether value and be within the restricted number ranges for the given bet type. The counter is incremented to generate a new ID before storing the new bet in the contract state and logs. The block for the spin RNG is set to three blocks in the future.

After the three-block waiting period is complete, the user can spin the roulette wheel to resolve their bet (Listing 11-7).

Listing 11-7. Resolving Roulette Bets

```
function spin (uint id) public {
    Bet storage bet = bets[id];
    require(msg.sender == bet.user);
    require(block.number >= bet.block);
    require(block.number <= bet.block + 255);

    bytes32 random = keccak256(block.blockhash(bet.block),
                                id);
    int landed = int(uint(random) % NUM_POCKETS) - 1;

    if (bet.betType == BetType.Color) {
        if (landed > 0 && COLORS[landed] == bet.choice)
            msg.sender.transfer(bet.amount * 2);
    }
    else if (bet.betType == BetType.Number) {
        if (landed == bet.choice)
            msg.sender.transfer(bet.amount * 35);
    }

    delete bets[id];
    Spin(id, landed);
}
```

Only the user who placed the bet can resolve it. The user must spin after the bet block has passed and within 255 blocks of the bet block so that the blockhash will be valid.

The trickiest part of this function is the random-number generation. Random bytes are generated by using the designated block's blockhash and the ID. The blockhash is unknown during the wager, and the ID is unique, so the outputted bytes are both unguessable and unique for every wager.

To turn the random bytes into a pocket on the roulette wheel, the bytes are converted to a uint, and the remainder operation is used to place the number from 0–37. That number is then converted to a signed int and decremented to get a roulette pocket, with a value of –1 standing in for the 00 pocket.

The bytes can't be converted directly to a signed int before the remainder operation because performing the remainder on a negative number would yield a negative number. To ensure that the remainder returns a positive number, the bytes must be cast to an unsigned integer first. Then the remainder output must be cast again to a signed integer so that it can take on a value of –1 if necessary.

After the winning pocket has been determined, payouts are doled out based on the bet type. For a color bet, if the winning pocket color is the same as the bet choice color, the user receives a 2× payout. For a number bet, if the winning pocket is the same as the bet choice, the user receives a 35× payout.

After payouts have been made, the bet is deleted so any payouts can't be reclaimed.

The contract contains two additional functions, one to fund the contract and one to kill it. Because they are the same as in Satoshi dice, they are not reproduced here.

In Exercise 11-2, you will have a chance to add additional features to the roulette contract.

EXERCISE 11-2. ROULETTE BET VARIETIES

So far, our roulette contract can accept only Number and Color bets. Modify the contract so that it can also accept Odd/Even bets, High/Low bets, and any other bet types you would like to add.

Summary

Ethereum gambling games allow for provably fair odds and gameplay. In this chapter, we created Satoshi dice and roulette game contracts for decentralized play on Ethereum. Both games are well-suited to blockchain gameplay because they are one-shot games with a wagering period that is separate from the one-shot gameplay.

We have now come to the end of this book. We have covered the basics of Solidity, dived deep into the intricacies of contract security, and written a series of increasingly complex Ethereum games that can be played wholly on-chain. Having successfully worked your way through the contracts and exercises in this book, you can consider yourself a qualified Solidity developer with the knowledge to tackle smart contract development at the highest level. Congratulations, and best of luck on your future Solidity endeavors!

References

Buterin, Vitalik. Vitalik's blog. Updated December 17, 2017.
`https://vitalik.ca/`

Daniel BC. Ethereum Blockchain Size. Updated February 26, 2018.
`http://bc.daniel.net.nz/`

Dannen, Chris. *Introducing Ethereum and Solidity: Foundations of Cryptocurrency and Blockchain Programming for Beginners*. Apress, 2017.

Ethereum Foundation. Ethereum Official Blog. Updated February 14, 2018.
`https://blog.ethereum.org/`

Ethereum Research. Technical Discussion Forum for Ethereum Research.
`https://ethresear.ch/`

Etherscan. The Ethereum Block Explorer. Updated February 26, 2018.
`https://etherscan.io/`

GitHub. Ethereum Improvement Proposals. Updated February 24, 2018.
`https://github.com/ethereum/EIPs`

GitHub. Mocha Test Framework. Updated February 20, 2018.
`https://github.com/mochajs/mocha/`

GitHub. Truffle Framework. Updated February 26, 2018.
`https://github.com/trufflesuite/truffle`

GitHub. Web3 JavaScript API. February 16, 2018.
`https://github.com/ethereum/wiki/wiki/JavaScript-API`

Medium. ConsenSys Medium Blog. Updated February 26, 2018.
`https://media.consensys.net/@ConsenSys`

Parity Technologies. Parity Ethereum Client. Last modified December 2017.
`www.parity.io`

Reddit. Ethereum Sub-Reddit. Updated February 26, 2018.
`http://reddit.com/r/ethereum`

© Kedar Iyer and Chris Dannen 2018
K. Iyer and C. Dannen, *Building Games with Ethereum Smart Contracts*,
https://doi.org/10.1007/978-1-4842-3492-1

REFERENCES

Solidity. Developer Documentation. Updated February 2018.
http://solidity.readthedocs.io

StackExchange. Ethereum StackExchange.
https://ethereum.stackexchange.com/

Truffle Framework. Ethereum Development Framework. 2018.
http://truffleframework.com/

YouTube. "Crockford on JavaScript—Chapter 2: And Then There Was JavaScript." History of JavaScript. September 20, 2011.
www.youtube.com/watch?v=RO1Wnu-xKoY#t=430

Zeppelin Solution. Zeppelin Blog. Updated February 23, 2018.
https://blog.zeppelin.solutions/

Index

A

Application binary
    interface (ABI), 11
Application-specific integrated
    circuits (ASICs), 130
Archive node, 34
Arithmetic operators, 83
Asymmetric key cryptography
    methods, 9
Attack vectors
    51% attack, 135–136
    breaking cryptography, 137–138
    network spamming, 136
    replay attacks, 138–139
    testnet attacks, 139–140

B

Bitcoin, 8, 130
Blockchain
    archive node, 20
    faucets, 36
    hard disk, 20
    Linux, 21
    macOS, 22
    programming tools, 23–25
    syncing, 20
    test network, 33
    truffle, 28–29
Block explorers, 13
Block reward, 2
Blocks, 1
Block validation rules, 132
Bytecode, 4

C

Chain split, 2
Coinbase transaction, 2
Coindash hack, 126
Command-line interface (CLI), 21
Commit-reveal puzzle
    claim prize, 222
    constructor, 220
    contract, 216
    Fibonacci sequence, 216
    guess function, 220
    isWinner function, 221
    reveal function, 221
Consensus, 132, 134
Contract address, 28
Contracts, 10
Contract security
    Coindash hack, 126
    Contract Creation code, 93

© Kedar Iyer and Chris Dannen 2018
K. Iyer and C. Dannen, *Building Games with Ethereum Smart Contracts*,
https://doi.org/10.1007/978-1-4842-3492-1